COLONIZATION
AND THE
WAMPANOAG STORY

COLONIZATION AND THE WAMPANOAG STORY

RACE TO THE TRUTH

Linda Coombs

CROWN BOOKS FOR YOUNG READERS
NEW YORK

Text copyright © 2023 by Race2Dinner and Linda Coombs
Cover art copyright © 2023 by Kristen Uroda
For interior image copyright information, see page 260.

Visit us on the Web! rhcbooks.com

Educators and librarians, for a variety of teaching tools,
visit us at RHTeachersLibrarians.com

Library of Congress Cataloging-in-Publication Data is available upon request.
ISBN 978-0-593-48043-4 (trade paperback) —
ISBN 978-0-593-48044-1 (lib. bdg.) — ISBN 978-0-593-48045-8 (ebook)

The text of this book is set in 12.5-point Adobe Garamond Pro.
Interior design by Jen Valero

Printed in the United States of America
10 9 8 7 6 5 4 3 2
First Edition

This book is dedicated to:

Turtle Island and all of Mother Earth, all the beings of the Earth, including the human.

The original people of Turtle Island, who have experienced what is described in this book whether in the world of the ancestors, the world we live in today, or in the Earth we leave for our future generations.

All the Indigenous people the world over, who have, still, and will experience the same processes of colonization.

My Wampanoag Nation family, for being and remaining who you are and keeping me who I am; those ancestors who lived through such experiences as related in this book and became our grandmothers and grandfathers; those ancestors who did not live through these experiences but are with us in spirit always; all you Wamps living today—Aquinnah, Mashpee, Herring Pond, Assonet—just know how much I love you and appreciate that you are still here. And for our children, and grandchildren, and their children and grandchildren.

Russell Means (Oglala Lakota) and Eddie Benton-Banai (Anishnaabe), whose influence, back in the AIM days of the early 1970s, set me on the path I have followed and the work that I have done.

The many, many people over the years who have been colleagues, friends, supporters, influencers, or my cousins—and patient, very patient: Dwight Peters (Mashpee Wampanoag), Joan Lester, Marge Bruchac (Abenaki), Lisa Brooks (Abenaki), Darius C. Coombs (Mashpee Wampanoag), Kristina Hook (Aquinnah Wampanoag), Everett "Tall Oak" Weeden (Wampanoag, Pequot), Alice Nash, Nanepashemet (Assonet Wampanoag), Ramona Peters (Mashpee Wampanoag), and Paulla Jennings (Narragansett). These are just a few of a great long list.

My immediate family: the Jeffers and the Belains (Aquinnah Wampanoag); Melvin S. Coombs, Sr. (Mashpee Wampanoag) (1948–1997), MMIP; my stepsons, Gustavus Ricciuiti and Melvin Coombs Jr., and their families; my son, Darius L. Coombs (Mashpee Wampanoag) (1986–2018); Guy Mason Jeffers (Aquinnah Wampanoag); and my grandchildren, Kayden Elijah Coombs and Jayla Maddison Coombs (both Mashpee Wampanoag).

Those who remember how big a word "respect" really is. Our stories continue.

CONTENTS

INTRODUCTION

This book is about Indigenous history, specifically that of the Wampanoag and other southern New England tribes. It focuses on Wampanoag territory as a point of first European contact and settlement, and the impacts of colonization on the Indigenous people of the region. We will look at this history and apply the following definition of racism to it.

RACISM:

1. A belief that race is a fundamental determinant of human traits and

capacities and that racial differences produce an inherent superiority of a particular race.

2. a) A doctrine or political program based on the assumption of racism and designed to execute its principles.

b) A political or social system founded on racism.

3. Racial prejudice or discrimination.

4. The systemic oppression of a racial group to the social, economic, and political advantage of another.

The book starts with a story, "When Life Was Our Own," which describes Wampanoag life before any European contact. The story was created to relate traditional Wampanoag culture, beliefs, practices, and values based on our oral traditions and research done over many years. There are no written sources of these early times, due to the processes of colonization described in the other parts of the book. An understanding of precontact life brings clarity to the impacts of colonization on Indigenous people.

The book outside of "When Life Was Our Own" is inclusive of all tribal nations in southern New England—Abenaki, Nipmuc, Pocumtuk, Mahican, Narragansett, Niantic, Pequot, Mohegan, and Wampanoag—as we all shared the same colonial experiences. The history sections start in the 1400s with events that occurred before 1620 and proceed chronologically through settlement and colonization to the present day.

This book relates history that happened, but which has been omitted or erased, or is distorted and stereotyped in history books today. The truth of history should be told because in this case, it is about the beginnings of America—the foundation America was built on. And the truth should be told. Period.

You will read a lot of things you've never heard about before, and they are pretty tough things. But this is not about blame or making anyone feel guilty or bad. That is not the purpose of this book. This is about readers gaining an understanding of what actually happened in the past. There are many wrongs in the past, but you can't fix something until you know what it is. We can't change what happened in the past, but we can decide to go forward in a better way, where there is equality and equity for all people.

While this book focuses on southern New England, the same formula of colonial processes was applied to other tribal nations across the rest of the country, as America expanded north, south, and west into their homelands.

CHAPTER 1

WHEN LIFE WAS OUR OWN: SPRING AND THE TIME OF THE NEW YEAR

GREETING THE DAY

Little Bird felt a slight breeze on her face and the sudden warmth of the morning sun, bidding her to open her eyes to a new day. Her body resisted rousing from the warm furs of the bed. Maybe just one more snuggle before getting up! Just yesterday, her family and many others had moved from the winter home to their summer cornfields. Sachem Corn Tassel, the leader of their village, had Little Bird's family return to the same field they'd planted in last year.

Little Bird was twelve now, and had helped her

Grandma Yellow Sky, Grandpa Singing Wolf, and Auntie Blue Heron carry all the bags and baskets that held everything to set up their summer household. There were dishes and cooking utensils; tools for tanning hides, woodworking, and stone knapping; axes and hoes for working in the garden; and bags of cordage (string and rope) used for making nets or weaving mats. It was only a mile's walk from the winter village, but it all seemed to get heavier as Little Bird walked along. Her arms felt like she had carried ten bags instead of only four!

Little Bird finally got one eye open and saw her Mom standing just outside the door. Smiling Dove was offering her morning prayers. Little Bird slid out from under the furs and quickly dressed. She went out and took Mom's hand, joining her in giving thanks for another morning. Her Dad was standing near the cornfield. Strong Bear faced east toward the ocean, his hand raised with his tobacco offering.

Little Bird looked across all the cornfields, which went as far as the eye could see. Everyone's houses were in the middle of their fields, where they could watch over their growing crops. People were coming out of their houses, offering prayers and getting fires started. Little Bird loved this first part of the morning. It was quiet and peaceful, and you could collect your thoughts for

Our prayers keep our connection to Mother Earth central in our minds.

the day. The smell of salt air was gently pungent, with only birdsong accenting the tranquil silence.

Back toward the winter village, the forest met the edges of the cornfields. The pine trees whispered their greetings as the wind rustled through their thick branches. Little Bird loved the sound of the wind rustling through the pines. She took a moment to just stand and listen.

SUMMER MOVE

Mom and Dad had come a few days earlier to check the frame of the house and make any necessary repairs. They had brought the bulrush and cattail mats that covered the frame so the rest of the family would have a roof over their heads when they arrived. Smiling Dove's field was close to a stream, at a place where the water tumbled down over the rocks like a tiny waterfall. A little pool formed at the bottom of the rocks, and sometimes you could find a bass or perch or trout resting from his travels. It was in a shady spot, deep enough to sit in on a hot sunny day, to splash around and wash the dust off from working in the garden. Last summer, when Strawberry, Little Bird's little sister, stood in the pool, the water came up to her neck. This year she was six, and so much taller, she figured the water would only be up to her chest!

Every day more people arrived, setting up and settling in for the summer. There was always so much to do! Some house frames needed repair; some needed to be replaced altogether. Smiling Dove's house was in good shape and didn't need a lot of work. The fields needed to be burned over and the soil turned. There were herring to be caught, Planting Ceremonies to hold, and corn to set in the earth. When all these things were done, it was time for the New Year Ceremonies, on the new moon in the Sowing Month When Corn Is Planted.

TIME TO EAT!

After morning prayers, Smiling Dove went back to their storage pit and brought out the rest of the dried food left from last fall. There was still a huge basket of corn for eating, as well as the seed corn. Little Bird and Strawberry helped her carry bags of dried beans, making two more trips to get all the baskets of dried squash and pumpkin, sunflower seeds, blueberries, and cranberries. There was even a small basket of smoked deer meat—maybe enough for a few meals.

Mom took everything into the house. She was going to cook inside today, as there was still an edge on the wind. Besides, the arbor over the summer kitchen just outside still needed new sheets of bark on its roof. The old ones were brittle and breaking, and their edges curling up. Smiling Dove stirred the embers of the fire back together, added some kindling, and got a good blaze going again. She took a medium-size clay kettle, filled it half full of water, and set it on three stones next to the main fire. Putting two handfuls of dried corn into the mortar, she began to crack it with the stone pestle.

Strawberry wanted to help so Mom showed her how to pick the heavy pestle up and drop it on the kernels to break them down into meal. Strawberry had to use both hands to hold the pestle even though it only had to be lifted a little ways. The mortar was deep enough to keep the corn from bouncing out when the pestle hit it. A very determined and zealous Strawberry, however, lifted the pestle too high, so when it dropped on the corn, kernels flew out, landing on the ground. Smiling Dove and Little Bird knelt and began picking them up. Neither had to say a word to Strawberry. She also started picking up the corn, realizing her mistake. She remembered the times when Grandma, Mom, Blue Heron, and others talked about corn and all food coming from living beings, how corn was a sacred plant to be handled with respect. The flyaway kernels were rinsed off and dried, to be used another day.

Meanwhile, Mom asked Little Bird to start a fire under the kettle, between its tripod of three rocks. The sticks and twigs burned into coals in just a few minutes. Little Bird kept feeding the fire, and very soon bubbles began to form on the water. Mom put three handfuls of dried beans into the pot.

She asked Little Bird to fill another kettle with more water at the spring. It was not far from the house, rippling out of the bank of the stream. By the time she got back, the beans were boiling steadily, and Mom had added some of Strawberry's cracked corn. She tamped the fire down a bit, so the pot would simmer. Strong Bear had made her a new stirring paddle of maple wood, carving a dove at the end of the handle. The girls could see how pleased Mom was with the paddle as she stirred the food, making sure nothing was sticking to the bottom of the kettle.

Ready for a piping hot breakfast on an early spring morning!

Strawberry had used all the strength in her arms to over-heft the pestle during her corn-pounding lesson. She leaned back on the bed to rest—her arms felt the way mud pies look when you make them in the rain. She closely watched Smiling Dove, who was grinding more kernels in the mortar. Strawberry realized that Mom really didn't put much effort into cracking the corn. She lifted the pestle a little ways, and let it drop. Lift and drop, lift and drop. She let the pestle do the work.

Little Bird didn't think she'd ever been hungrier and couldn't wait to eat! They'd had a big supper when they got to the fields, which clearly wasn't enough to hold her until breakfast.

She helped Mom mix the cornmeal with hot water and dried blueberries, making dough for boiled bread. They formed the dough into little round cakes and dropped them into the simmering pot of stew when it was just about done. Finally! Breakfast was ready! Little Bird waited patiently, helping Mom serve bowls of stew and boiled bread to Grandma and Grandpa and to her Dad. Then Mom gave Little Bird and Strawberry their breakfast, before making a dish for herself. No one started eating until a prayer of thanks was given, to the corn, the beans, the water, the blueberries—which was hot and satisfying on a cool spring morning.

INTO THE CEDAR SWAMP

After breakfast, Strong Bear and his brother Tall Pine met with a group of the men. They were deciding who would go into the cedar swamp to gather saplings for the house frames that needed repair, and who would begin burning over the cornfields, getting them ready for planting.

Strong Bear went with the men to the swamp. The one nearest them extended over such a huge area that people from several villages harvested from it.

for centuries, knowing that the time to harvest was in the spring when the sap rose in the trees. This is what allowed the poles to be bent into the house frames without breaking. Upon entering the swamp, the men chose the area to begin cutting.

First and foremost, they offered prayers, thanking the trees for the gift of their lives so the people could build homes. They also showed respect by cutting in a way that encouraged the growth of new saplings. The men tended the areas they cut so that conditions in the swamp were ideal for the trees to flourish. Swamp cedar grows tall and straight, with most branches near the tops of the trees. The limbs and seed cones were trimmed off and left to produce new saplings.

The cut poles could be thirty feet long, or more. When the men brought them back to the planting sites, they were put in the river to keep them supple and bendable. The first job was to peel the bark off, and everyone, even some of the little kids, pitched in to help. This kept bugs from burrowing into the frames of the houses, and the bark itself had many uses. The outer bark was separated from the smooth inner layer and used as tinder to start fires. The inner bark became lashing for the house frames, mats for the floors, and also, baskets.

A complete, brand-new frame could be built in a day, although Smiling Dove's house only needed new lashings in some spots to hold the frame together. The house really didn't need much work after the winter.

No parts of the trees were ever wasted. Cedar, like tobacco, is a sacred plant, and the leaves were used in ceremony.

BURNING THE FIELDS

Tall Pine and his family lived near Strong Bear, in the next cornfield over. He met with some of the other men to begin the plan for burning and clearing the fields, including those that would lie fallow and not be planted this year. This was done in spring and fall. The ashes were worked back into the mounds, enriching the soil to help the corn and other vegetables grow. When ready for planting, the fields looked like a grid of foot-high hills spaced evenly apart, stretching as far as the eye could see.

This was such a good time of year! Each family had a large planting field, about an acre or more for their corn. Everyone helped in all the gardens. Men, women, and children worked together, sometimes singing, always laughing. The women cooked lots of food, and everyone would take a break and sit in he shade to have a meal. People always carried their own bowl and spoon for just such occasions. Cleanup for a hundred people was easy, as everyone washed their own dishes after they ate!

HERRING PEEPERS, HERRING TIME

Everyone checked the river every day, watching for the herring to come up on their spawning runs. The people used them for food and also for fertilizer in the gardens. The herring peepers, little frogs who emerge from their muddy winter hibernation in early, early spring, had been heard for weeks now. Little Bird and her Dad spent many evenings sitting quietly and listening to the comforting rhythm of their chirping chorus, carrying the promise of spring.

Strawberry could never figure out how the herring knew which river to come back up to the pond they were born in. Little Bird explained this to her every year, but so far it was still a big mystery! Strawberry would be six soon, so maybe this was the year that she would come to this understanding. Everyone learns in their own time. Little Bird noticed, however, that Strawberry had no trouble understanding when the herring were roasted and juicy over the fire! She was already adept at removing the many bones so she didn't choke as she swallowed tender morsels of her fish dinner. She wanted to be just like her Dad and her Grandpas, who could eat and maneuver the bones out the sides of their mouths into a wondrous, woven net-looking . . . thing!

The herring being so bony was the reason they made good fertilizer for the corn mounds. When they were running heavily, the men would collect them with dip nets, and carry basketfuls to the cornfields. Of course, this was always done with proper ceremony, acknowledging the fish that were giving up their lives, so everyone could grow their corn. Fertilizing was not done every year, but only when the soil needed it. Otherwise, only enough herring for food was caught.

The men worked very hard with the river. They cleared fallen branches from certain places so the water could flow freely, but they left brush in other places so the fish could rest there, hidden from hawk-view.

The men also helped in the gardens, digging holes for the fish fertilizer with stone-bladed hoes, then hilling the earth into mounds. Smiling Dove's fields didn't need fertilizer this year, and Little Bird and Strawberry didn't mind not having to handle the slippery fish! Putting two fish in each hole in the entire garden took hundreds of fish. That was a lot of slipperiness to then hill the mounds up over! Actually, Little Bird didn't even mind this work. Preparing the garden was very

The herring return home to their birth pond,
while the men hear the song of the herring peepers.

pleasant in the spring sunshine and gentle breezes.
She loved the feeling of working with her hands in the
warm earth—like being home, connected, knowing
you're exactly where you're supposed to be.

CORN MOTHER: PLANTING TIME

Smiling Dove, along with Little Bird and Strawberry,
met with the women from all the other families. The
clan mothers gathered them together to organize
the Spring Planting Ceremonies. The women's connection to the corn was honored, as both are female
spirits. The corn, beans, squashes, pumpkins, melons,

13

and sunflowers are acknowledged and given thanks for the food and nourishment that they provide. Their lives make it possible for ours to continue.

During the ceremonies, Little Bird always looked forward to hearing her Grandma sing all the different songs. She had a deep, rich voice, and Little Bird—especially when she was smaller—would sit in her lap, resting her head against Grandma's chest. She could feel the song resonating, like it was rising right out of Grandma's heart. Sometimes an eagle or a hawk would fly overhead, shrilling in complement to the ladies' singing.

The day of the new moon had come, and people had been watching for signs that it was safe to plant. When the shadbush blooms and the leaves of the oak were the size of a mouse's ear, there would be no more frost. The ground was warm and ready to bring forth new life. It was time to plant!

Everyone's field only took a day or so to plant, as the women and children all helped each other. Planting sticks made small holes in the tops of each mound, and four kernels of corn were dropped in. A swipe of the foot covered soil over the hole, and the women could quickly get the seed into the ground. Of course, some people were still working on their aim with the corn seed. Little Bird had become pretty proficient at age twelve and hardly ever had to retrieve an overshot kernel. Little Strawberry, on the other hand, spent more time stooping and scooping the seeds that missed the holes than she did remaining upright! She had planted far fewer hills than the other girls. Little Bird could tell, though, that she was doing better than last year. She waited for her sister and saw that some girls were also purposefully going slower so that Strawberry would not feel bad because she was not as fast. After all, it is the learning and working together that matters—not a competition to see who is fastest. This was something children learned from the time they were born.

So now, after only a few days, everyone's corn had been set. The men had planted the tobacco gardens with the tiny seeds from last year's harvest. Tobacco was a very important plant. It was smoked socially when guests came in, and was used in all ceremonies. The men had also repaired or rebuilt the corn watch towers in the middle of the fields. All the kids went to work then, sitting up there at dawn and again at dusk. Their job was to scare the birds and small animals away from digging up the seed or newly sprouted corn. They yelled and threw sticks at them, all the while worrying should they injure a little bird. Especially Little Bird! She was given that name when she was three because a tiny chickadee landed right on her toes when she was sitting outside one day. He perched on her foot for a while, eyeing her confidently as the little girl sat mesmerized. She slowly reached out, hoping he might hop on her hand. But off he flew to his next destination—and away from the toddler's grasp!

It always seemed to take forever for the baby corn to sprout through the soil. Seeing the tiny plants emerge from the earth as a result of your own work was such a good feeling! The kids all got very serious about their jobs in the corn watch towers. The work was just beginning. When the corn plants were as tall as your hand from wrist to fingertips, it was time to plant the other vegetables—the beans, squashes, pumpkins, and also the melons and sunflowers. The many types of beans and squashes, pumpkins and melons were planted in the mounds with the corn. Sunflowers were planted around the edges of the garden, to stand like sentinels watching over the crops.

While the different types of squashes were planted separately so they wouldn't mix, people didn't worry about the beans. They got planted together, stored together, cooked together, and the best part—eaten together! The beans seemed to know what they were doing—they always grew their own kind even if four different ones were planted in the same mound. This was another mystery for Strawberry to ponder! But she carried on and helped the other girls, spacing four beans evenly around each mound, halfway down the sides. At the same time, four squash, pumpkin, or melon seeds were planted around the base of each mound. Strawberry—well, all the kids—couldn't wait for the harvest, when the sweet, juicy pink melons would be ready to eat. So refreshing on a hot end-of-summer day!

NEW YEAR CEREMONIES

But it was a long ways from melon-harvesting time! It was still spring, with plants flowering and trees sprouting tiny, new green leaves. The soil in the garden was warm to small bare feet. The folks who had to build new house frames were finishing up the job now, fresh strips of cedar bark binding new poles together. Everyone's garden had been planted and was carefully being watched over. The first work of spring and summer was completed! It was time to prepare for the New Year Ceremonies.

Here was one situation that was not a mystery to Strawberry! She already understood why spring was called the New Year! It made complete sense! There are new baby animals and birds, the herring come home to have their babies, the trees have brand-new leaves, and all the plants and flowers come alive again and sprout from the earth after the long winter. Everything in the world is new in spring—so it is the New Year.

New Year was an important ceremony, with great gatherings of people from all over coming together to pray and give thanks to honor new life. After the ceremonies, there was feasting and visiting. It was a time when people gathered with friends and family they might not see very often. Everyone ate and sang and danced. There were dances and songs done only during ceremony; and after, those for the enjoyment of being together. The singers got everyone up and moving with the social dance songs. The singers each had two sticks carved with beautiful designs, keeping rhythm on a log or folded hides. Sometimes the singing and dancing went on all night!

The aromas coming from the cook areas were overwhelmingly delicious, as huge feast kettles bubbled with soups and stews! Everyone brought food to cook, and some people had turkeys and geese roasting over the fires. Strawberry wished she could help cook, but she was still too little to stir the feast kettles. Even though she had grown (a lot!), she could barely see into the huge pots!

Little Bird helped her Auntie Blue Heron pack a

fish with firewood, adding more as it burned down. It took an experienced fish-baker to tell when the clay was dried through and the fish done.

Other people dug pits on the beach, building huge fires, burning them down to the hottest coals. They collected rockweed, a seaweed that has little bubbles that contain seawater. Layers of rockweed went on the hot coals, making the bubbles release their water as steam. Lobsters, clams, quahogs, and mussels were piled on the rockweed, and more piled on top of them. Old mats were laid over the pits to hold the steam in as it cooked and flavored the food.

For a while, Little Bird couldn't find Strawberry anywhere! She wasn't in the house. She wasn't with a group of children who divided their time between dancing and running around and playing. She wasn't in the corn watch tower. She wasn't with Auntie Blue Heron and her family. These cousins were already asleep back at their house. Finally, she could see her Uncle Tall Pine in the light of the fires. He was carrying Strawberry in his arms, and she was sound asleep! She had gone back to his house with those cousins, where climbing onto a bearskin on the bed cued her eyes that it was time for them to shut! Tall Pine laid Strawberry down in her own bed, covering her with Mom's favorite beaver fur robe. One Strawberry mystery solved!

It had been a long, full, and wonderful day. Little Bird bid her Uncle good night as they passed on the path. She was so tired, she thought she might have to lie down right there for a nap so she would have enough energy to get home to bed. She could see the fire glowing in the house, but it may as well have been on the moon. This had been a great beginning of summer!

Sending prayers to Creator.

CHAPTER 2

CREATING COLONIES: MORE THAN A NEW PLACE TO LIVE

SOME BACKGROUND INFORMATION AND CONTEXT (NEVER FORGET THE CONTEXT!)

This section will discuss three episodes in history that occurred before 1620. These paved the way for the Pilgrims to settle in America. They are the Doctrine of Discovery; the impacts of Christopher Columbus's voyages; and the PPP—Pre-Pilgrim Patterns—which happened along coastal southern New England.

The Doctrine of Discovery opened the door through which Columbus sailed at the beginning of

WAMPANOAG TERRITORY

This map shows the homeland of the Wampanoag people. Shown are some of the sixty-nine original villages.

the "Age of Exploration." Everyone, of course, has heard of Christopher Columbus. He is credited for "sailing the ocean blue in 1492"; for being a knowledgeable and skilled navigator; and—last but not least—for discovering America! Not so well known is his treatment of the Indigenous people into whose lands he entered, and the terrible fates they suffered at his hands. The PPP were a series of events including epidemics, kidnapping, and enslavement, all of which had life-altering impacts on the Indigenous people of the region. These events nevertheless enabled the Pilgrims to settle in the Wampanoag Homeland, on the site of the village of Patuxet, which the English renamed Plimoth (Plymouth).

These things have been intentionally and completely left out of the history books, in order to create a shining, positive image of the European settlement of America.

But these things actually did happen. To leave them out is not presenting the truth of history. This is damaging and hurtful to the people left out, and also to those who don't learn the truth.

People don't do things like this to those they consider equal. Equality cannot exist when such things happen.

DOCTRINE OF DISCOVERY: WHOSE IDEA WAS THIS?

The Doctrine of Discovery is a series of Papal Bulls—bulletins or documents written by the Pope—that were issued from the time of the Crusades in the 1200s until 1493.

They essentially declared that non-Christian people were the enemies of Christian people; that non-Christians were less than human; that Christians had the right to enter the countries of non-Christians and take their lands and the resources of that land; and that Christians could enslave non-Christians and otherwise treat them as less than human.

According to Pope Nicholas in 1452, Christians

could "capture, vanquish, and subdue the saracens, pagans, and other enemies of Christ," "put them into perpetual slavery," and "take all their possessions and property."

Let's think about this. How does not being Christian, or worshipping differently, make people less than human? What is the issue with people worshipping in their own way? The Christian religion is based on the teachings of Jesus Christ two thousand years ago. Jesus acknowledged the Godliness in all people, regardless of race, gender, skin color, way of worshipping, or way of life. Does the Doctrine of Discovery follow the teachings of Jesus Christ? Why did the Pope back then think it was right or necessary to create the Doctrine of Discovery?

What does "When Life Was Our Own" say? At the very beginning, what is the first thing Little Bird does when she gets up? How many times do people, either individually, as family, or in community, give thanks, offer prayers, or have ceremony? How does imposing beliefs on others compare to the way people treat each other here?

Wampanoag and other Indigenous people were not Christians, but neither were they "godless savages" as European people called them. Giving thanks, offering prayer, and holding ceremony were ways that

Indigenous people acknowledged and honored the Creator, and therefore Creation: the earth, the natural world, the systems that make the world work the way it was created to.

CHRISTOPHER COLUMBUS: WHO DISCOVERED WHOM?

Christopher Columbus is hailed for discovering the "New World." Indigenous people assert that lands already having millions of people living there cannot be "discovered" by someone else. This effectively denies our origins and continued existence in our homelands in North, Central, and South America.

And yet, this *belief* about Columbus has been given more credence than the centuries-long histories and ancient cultures of Indigenous people. Why is his reputation more important than the lives and histories of these millions of people?

In spite of Columbus's fame, his treatment of the Indigenous people whose lands he entered in the Caribbean islands has basically been omitted from the teaching of history.

In his logbook, he tells of coming to an island called Guanahaní and being greeted by the Indigenous people there. Coming to the beach to meet the ship, they were welcoming and joyous, bringing food and gifts.

Living in a tropical climate, these people wore very little clothing. The Europeans gave them the negative label, therefore, of being "primitive," since "civilized" people fully clothe themselves. Columbus and the ship's crew had themselves covered from the neck down and the wrists and ankles up. Everything met in the middle under the metal armor they felt they needed to wear. They apparently missed the memo about wearing sensible shoes and dressing for the weather! The people from the island, who had lived there for thousands of years, knew the climate and designed their wardrobes accordingly.

Once onshore, Columbus, upon approaching these people, extended the blade of his sword. A Guanahaní man, not knowing what this weapon was, took the blade in his hand and cut himself.

The Guanahaní had no knowledge of such weapons. In contrast to the concept of weaponry, they were totally welcoming to these strangers, offering them refreshment and gifts. Columbus observed these traits, commenting that these people were "guileless": open, honest, welcoming, glad to see these newcomers— without hidden agendas. Because of these (normally considered) positive traits, Columbus stated, "They ought to make good and skilled servants, for they repeat very quickly whatever we say to them. I think they can easily be made Christians, for they seem to have no religion."

What is the key word in Columbus's comment? ". . . they **seem** to have no religion." Why did Columbus assume he could make such a judgment? How did he come to determine the Guanahaní had no religion? He had just stepped off the boat, and neither he nor his crew bothered to stop and take any time to get to know these folks. He did not treat them with the respect offered equal human beings, but rather, operated from his assumptions.

Over the course of his four voyages, Columbus enslaved thousands of Indigenous people throughout the Caribbean islands. He wanted them to find gold, which would make the countries that he was sailing for rich, not to mention himself. When the people of the various islands did not, or could not, find gold to fill the quotas they were assigned, they were subjected to mental, emotional, and physical torture, and were maimed and mutilated.

LET'S THINK ABOUT THIS:

1. Was Columbus following the directives of the Doctrine of Discovery?

2. Regardless of any papal directive, was it right for Columbus to treat these Indigenous people the way that he did?

3. Was it Columbus's right or responsibility to determine whether the Guanahaní were "primitive" or "civilized"?

4. How do Columbus's assumptions compare with the activities in the "Greeting the Day" and "New Year Ceremonies" sections of "When Life Was Our Own"?

5. Can you find any similarities between the Guanahaní (granted, from a short quote) and the people in "When Life Was Our Own"?

6. Why didn't the Guanahaní have any knowledge of European-style weapons?

CHAPTER 3

WHEN LIFE WAS OUR OWN: SUMMER—TENDING TO CORN MOTHER

T he corn was planted, cedar poles collected, houses built or repaired—the work of settling into the summer homes was complete. Even the crows and the blackbirds seemed to be taking some time off from their attempted garden raids! At least for a moment. . . . Several children sat on the corn watch, swinging their legs over the edge of the platform, chins in their hands—it was unusual to have no one to scare out of the fields! The kids figured they should enjoy the lull while it lasted!

The river nearby flowed into the ocean, the soft pungency of salt air filling little noses, joined by the fragrance of wild roses. Little Bird thought that combination of scents was her favorite in all the world. Nothing could compare to the scent of a pine forest, or that of a wood fire wafting through the air. She loved the smell of freshwater as breezes carried it from the ponds and lakes. And the earth of the forest floor in the fall . . . but still, her favorite was the salt air and roses.

Summer was really starting to heat up now. The fields in the newly planted earth had their own dusty scent in the hot air. Things would change quickly as the corn plants sprouted. Then the real work would begin—scaring off the crows, blackbirds, geese, squirrels, raccoons, and many other nibblers, diggers, and rooters! At night, the Dads walked around the edges of the fields, bows and arrows in hand, making sure deer wouldn't invite themselves in for a midnight snack!

Life is good in the summer villages, tending corn,
catching fish, feeling the warmth of the earth and
the refreshing coolness of the water.

SUMMER'S FIRST GIFT

Full summer had arrived! The trees were fully leafed out, and the world was dressed in fresh new green only seen in this early part of the season. It was already time to gather strawberries. The clans came together for ceremony to give thanks for the first fruit of the season. Everyone looked forward to picking time! Whether by the bowlful, added to boiled bread, or made into a pudding or a cool drink, their fresh sweetness was a welcome addition to any meal. Every meal!

Little Bird and Strawberry, with some of their cousins from neighboring cornfields, Punkinseed and River, Woodchuck and Red Dawn, headed out early to go picking. Punkinseed and River were the children of Blue Heron and her husband, Walks in the Moonlight, and Woodchuck and Red Dawn's parents were Tall Pine and his wife, Stands Strong. The cousins headed to the field that their families always went to first, each carrying their own basket. They walked half the morning to get there, and everyone was hungry when they arrived. They had each brought food with them, and, choosing a grassy spot to sit, the kids laid out everything to share. There was boiled bread with last fall's dried cranberries; boiled bread made with parched cornmeal, or nocake, with last summer's dried blueberries; and then there was no-cake with hominy corn. After thinking about it, and reviewing the spread before them, everyone thought they would try the boiled bread—very satisfying stick-to-your-ribs food!

Before eating, they held hands in a circle to give thanks. Red Dawn, as the oldest cousin, offered to-bacco and a prayer of thanksgiving for the food be-fore them, and for the strawberries they were about to pick. The field they were in was very large, stretching as far as the eye could see. Way in the distance, the kids could see dots of white blossoms and red fruit, ripe for picking.

As huge as the field was, they walked by the first patches of strawberries, and went on to farther ones. Each child chose a spot a little ways from the others, and intently set about picking. They walked carefully so as not to step on any strawberry plants. Everyone picked as far as they could reach, then moved to an-other spot. They were very careful to leave some areas untouched, either for others to gather, or for the birds, and to ensure there would always be strawber-ries. They had been taught this their entire lives, and it was just the natural thing to do.

The cousins picked for a while, taking breaks to sit

in the shade or go to the nearby spring for a cool drink of water. The wild strawberries were tiny, not much bigger than a bean, but mouthwateringly sweet! After a while, everyone's basket was getting pretty full. Somehow, Strawberry's never seemed to fill more than halfway. Yet interestingly, her cheeks and fingers were much redder than when she entered the field! Not to mention a couple of red blotches on the front of her clothing. The other children smiled and chuckled, as Strawberry once again lived up to her name. Both Little Bird and Red Dawn gently reminded her that she should save some to bring home to Mom and Grandma. And that she should probably save some room for the raspberries and blackberries that would be ripening soon! And then later in the summer, the

The people give thanks for the first gift of summer.

blueberries! Then the black cherries! Then the grapes. So many berries, so little picking time!

Later, the children made their way home, with everyone going back to Little Bird's house. She and Strawberry gave their baskets to their Mom. She thanked the girls for gathering the fruit but smiled at Strawberry's half-full basket and red face and hands. She and Dad laughed, teasing her that perhaps next time, she should bring a smaller basket that would be easier to fill. Mom offered to paint some designs on her dress to match the strawberry stains. Strawberry laughed at their jokes, too, but she didn't miss the point that the strawberry picking was done for the whole family, not just herself.

THE OCEAN'S GIFTS

The men spent most of their time in the summer at the water, fishing and shellfishing. Strong Bear and Tall Pine took all the boys, River, Woodchuck, and Red Dawn over to the estuary, the mouth of the river. They traveled in two dugout canoes that could each hold three or four people. They built a camp back near the woods, as they would be there for a few days. Smiling Dove and Stands Strong had packed some dry corn and beans for them, as well as some cornmeal. They could gather fresh strawberries, onions and garlic, and lots of new greens for their soups. There were plenty of clams and quahogs, and bass and perch to make a meal a feast! And it was just about the time for the bluefish to run! The boys all looked forward to catching a huge blue to roast over the fire!

Strong Bear and Tall Pine led the boys to the maple swamp. They cut saplings to repair the fish weir that had been built in the estuary. It needed a good number of new upright poles after winter freezes and spring torrents had broken older ones. They peeled the bark and their Dads showed them how to set the poles firmly into the river bottom. This was a lot of work that took most of the day!

They went back to camp, hungry and ready for dinner. Strong Bear, River, and Woodchuck laid out a firepit and got a blaze going. Strong Bear put on a kettle to make soup, and the boys went to collect greens to add to the pot. Tall Pine and Red Dawn headed one of the boats into open water to look for that bluefish! They had plenty of twisted basswood bark line and newly made fishhooks of deer bone and antler. They also brought along a dip net in case they needed to scoop up a bluefish who was not thrilled with the idea of becoming dinner!

While Tall Pine and Red Dawn were fishing, Woodchuck and River dived into the ocean waves.

The salt water was refreshing and relaxing after the hard work of the day! The boys began to feel around the ocean bottom with their feet. It didn't take long to unearth a good number of quahogs to add to tonight's menu. It was low tide when they came out of the water, and they walked along the shore, looking for small holes in the firm sand. Digging at these spots, they added clams to the menu as well. River and Woodchuck could hardly wait to eat! There was nothing like fresh shellfish after the long winter! They looked out and saw Tall Pine and Red Dawn returning with a beautiful bluefish that was almost as long as River's arm. He held his arm against its length (just for accuracy!), always amazed at the sparkling iridescence of the fish's scales glistening in the sunlight.

Tall Pine and Red Dawn gutted the bluefish and put him on a spit. While they were gone, Strong Bear got a good fire going, which now had a big bed of glowing red coals, ready to roast the fish. River and Woodchuck rinsed the sand off the shellfish and put them in a clay kettle and filled it with water. River added a handful of cornmeal to the water to cause the shellfish to spit out any sand they had inside them. Crunchy clams are hard on the teeth!

All the boys helped Strong Bear keep an eye on the bluefish, turning the spit so it would cook evenly.

Roasting seemed to take forever to the hungry boys! In actuality, it was nowhere near forever before the fish was almost done. There was just enough time to cook the shellfish—into the soup they went, shells and all, adding their salty flavor.

Finally everything was done! Tall Pine lifted the spit from over the fire, and Red Dawn used the stirring paddle to push the steaming fish into the serving bowl. As the fish cooled, they stood in a circle and gave thanks to all the beings that were now their dinner, grateful for the abundance of food. Everyone filled their own bowls with soup and took a big piece of fish. Woodchuck especially loved the meat that came from the cheeks of the bluefish. It came out in rounds, like little neat treats, two or three bites each. Both men and boys ate heartily after the long day's work. No one spoke a word for quite a while—not being able to get the food in fast enough!

Before long, though, everyone was full. Strong Bear put away the rest of the fish, saving it for breakfast. The skeleton had a lot of meat left on it and would be a great start to the morning meal. There was no soup or shellfish left at all. Red Dawn washed out the kettle at the shore and set it back on its three stones. His Dad took all the shells a little ways up the beach to dump them into the shell heap. This place had been used as a fish camp for centuries, and everyone always put their shells and bones in the same heap. It was so old that the bottom shells had disintegrated into the earth, and the ones on the surface were bleached by sun and storms and thousands of winters.

Everyone washed his own bowl and spoon. Everyone, that is, except River. He had leaned against one of the frame poles of their shelter and fallen fast asleep— his bowl in his lap and spoon still in his hand. He did get that last bite down before sleep overtook him! Red Dawn washed his dishes, while Tall Pine carried him inside the shelter and laid him on the furs, to continue his journey into dreamland.

Everyone else sat around the fire, talking softly, as the sun began to set. They discussed their plans for fishing and shellfishing over the following days. Smiling Dove, Stands Strong, and the younger girls, Strawberry and Punkinseed, would be coming out in a day or so. They would be smoking and drying most of the clams, quahogs, and mussels that they and the men would be harvesting. They would also preserve some of the fish they caught, to be stored away for winter meals.

The women and girls arrived late the next day, bringing more corn, beans, and cornmeal. They made sleeping areas for themselves and set about making dinner. They had also brought bags of string. Shellfish as cooked and removed from the shell, put on string like a food necklace—only longer—and hung over the fire to smoke. Once completely dried, the fish could last for many months.

Everyone got up early the next day. The women made breakfast while the men went and started digging quahogs, mussels, and clams. They dug for most of the day. Red Dawn and River showed the younger children how to feel out the quahogs with their feet, and to dig clams where the little holes appeared at the shore. The sun was hot on their brown skin, but they could always take a cool dunk in the ocean when needed. Everyone was getting a lot of shellfish! Smiling Dove and Stands Strong steadily steamed them, putting their meat into a large bowl. They showed the younger girls how to string the shellfish and hang them over the smoking racks. When the fires were going good, the women laid dry corncobs on the coals, which would smoke heavily to dry the fish.

Strawberry and Punkinseed each did a few strings, but then decided they had learned enough for one day. They headed for the river, where Punkinseed pointed out a group of little fish. They were using their bodies and tails to sweep away sand in the shallow of the river. Punkinseed explained that they were creating nests where they would lay their eggs and have their babies. She said these fish were called punkinseeds. Strawberry's eyes widened as she realized they had the same name as her cousin! Her cousin explained that she had gotten that name two years ago, when she had stopped some boys in a canoe from pulling up into a spot where the punkinseeds were laying their eggs.

Strawberry listened intently, seriously taking in her cousin's words. The thought of the boat crushing the fish and obliterating the nests was very disturbing! She was so glad Punkinseed had been able to stop the boat in time!

The girls headed back to camp, where the men had just finished repairing the large net they would use at the weir. The boys were all busy repairing the dip nets with basswood bark cordage. Strawberry and Punkinseed watched them for a while, until the boys asked them to walk down the beach to look for horseshoe crab shells with the tails. When they finished the nets, they would collect thin, straight saplings, first offering some tobacco, cedar, sage, or sweetgrass, or some cornmeal, to pray and give thanks when taking a life. The boys needed saplings that were at least as tall as Red Dawn, trimmed of bark and branches. The horseshoe crab tails would be attached to them with bark string and hide glue, and Red Dawn, Woodchuck, and River would all have new fishing spears!

CHAPTER 4

PPP: PRE-PILGRIM PATTERNS

The PPP describes three significant occurrences that happened before 1620: the Age of Exploration, kidnapping and slavery along the east coast, and the Great Dying, an epidemic killing tens of thousands. These things laid the groundwork for European settlement and colonization in what became America.

THE AGE OF EXPLORATION

The Age of Exploration began in the 1400s and lasted into the 1600s. Probably the most well-known explorer during this time is Christopher Columbus, who made four voyages between 1492 and 1504 into the Caribbean area.

Columbus was one of many explorers, part of a continual flow of ships sailing under the flags of many European countries. All hoped to find gold or other forms of wealth to enrich those countries. England, the Netherlands, and France were in competition with one another to establish colonies and claim territory in the land they named "America."

Following in Columbus's footsteps, many, many European ships sailed into what is now the southern New England–Long Island area, beginning about one hundred years before the Pilgrims settled in Plymouth in 1620. Giovanni da Verrazzano was the first explorer to arrive in Narragansett territory in what is now Rhode Island in 1524. We know this because he kept a journal of his travels, the people he met, and the lands that he saw. Many of these explorers also wrote such information down. Note that Verrazzano sailed into Narragansett Bay only thirty-two years after Columbus's first voyage.

Some of the other explorers at this time were Bartholomew Gosnold, who sailed around Buzzards Bay and Martha's Vineyard (1602); Martin Pring, who came into Plymouth Harbor (1603); Samuel de Champlain, who sailed between Massachusetts and Maine (1605); and Thomas Dermer, who went to Cape Cod and Maine (1619).

The ships were coming out of Europe for four basic reasons. They came to explore the region, meaning to look for land to establish colonies in Indigenous people's territories. They came to trade a variety of goods with Indigenous people in exchange for furs and other things. They came to fish, coming here during the summer months and leaving before winter set in so they had time to get home. And they came to capture and enslave Indigenous people.

The goal of European countries in establishing colonies was gaining "power" and building empire, to be the greatest country in the world. Trading and fishing were essentially extractive activities, gleaning the "resources" from the land or water (fur, timber, sassafras, fish) to be turned into wealth and profit. Enslavement is treatment that occurs when some people see others as less than human, or see themselves as superior.

Europeans essentially didn't acknowledge they were entering the countries and cultures of different Indigenous nations. They often affronted the people they were attempting to negotiate with, treating them from preconceived notions of being "backward" or "primitive." In the fur trade, Indigenous people were the providers. As Europeans increased their demand for furs, this disrupted the balance of nature with the animals and the earth. This in turn disrupted Indigenous peoples' ways of life.

This competition and quest for "power," empire, and wealth continues today. It is framed as "progress." Yet so many people live in poverty, endure many types of deadly diseases, and suffer from social or racial injustices or other inequities. The natural world that still provides everything we need is on the brink of destruction. How does the attitude that drives this quest compare with that displayed toward other people and the earth in "When Life Was Our Own"?

KIDNAPPING AND SLAVERY

During this time, certain ship captains began kidnapping Wampanoag men and those of other tribal nations along the coast. Sailors invited them aboard their ships under the pretense of trading, then lifted anchor and sailed away. The men were prisoners, stolen from their families and homes.

They were taken to England and Spain to be sold into slavery and paraded through the streets as "novelties," something for the people of Europe to gawk at as curiosities—not as human beings. Imagine how these men must have felt when they realized their

Wampanoag men being kidnapped to be sold into slavery in Europe.

situation: they would never see their children, parents, wives, relatives, or communities and homelands again. What a terrible shock for all their families when they realized their men were gone—just disappeared forever!

As far as is known, only two people, at least among the Wampanoag, ever made it back home. One was Squanto, or Tisquantum, from the Wampanoag town of Patuxet. He was taken in 1614 and returned in 1619. Squanto is well known for being the great helper and translator for the Pilgrims. But he was a man in a very difficult situation. While he was in Europe, all connection with home and family was lost. He was returned just after the Great Dying, which we'll learn about next, to find not only his family

Squanto and other Wampanoag
men captured and held below deck
on a ship bound for Europe.

gone but his entire village wiped out. Imagine how he must have felt! Squanto died in 1622 of a fever, perhaps not yet thirty years old.

The other person to return from Europe was a man named Epenow from the Aquinnah Wampanoag people on what is now Martha's Vineyard island in Massachusetts. Epenow was taken in 1611 and returned in 1614. Epenow's story is also a difficult one. He figured out what the English valued more than anything in life: gold! He told them that there was gold on his island home of Capawack (Martha's Vineyard), and that if they brought him back, he would show them where it was. The English believed him and eagerly set sail for Capawack, but they did not trust Epenow, and when nearing the island, they shackled him and dressed him in a large, loose English shirt. They reasoned that if Epenow should attempt to jump ship and swim to shore, they could grab the shirt to prevent his escape. But over the side he did go, shackles, shirt, and all. Many people in canoes had come out to see what the ship was about and, recognizing Epenow, helped him ashore. A skirmish ensued, and the ship's captain was wounded, later passing away in Virginia. Epenow, for his part, was back in his home, and later became sachem, or chief, of Aquinnah.

THE GREAT DYING

Between 1616 and 1618, a huge plague struck along the east coast, from what is now Maine down to what is now Massachusetts. Among the Wampanoag and other tribal nations in this area, entire villages died during this sickness. Notice this was only two years before the Pilgrims settled on the site of Patuxet.

The Great Dying is known to have been brought by European fishermen, who left two men behind on the Maine coast when their ship returned to Europe. This sickness affected several different nations of Indigenous people, including Abenaki (Penna-cook), down into Wampanoag territory. From coastal Maine, it swept a fifteen-mile-wide path as it hurtled south. When it hit Patuxet, it turned inland, sweeping through the middle of Wampanoag Country, stopping at Narragansett Bay.

Everywhere the plague touched experienced a 75 percent to 90 percent death rate. Prior to this illness, the Wampanoag nation had sixty-nine villages or towns. Wampanoag historians estimate that each village averaged about one thousand people, so approximately seventy thousand people in our entire nation.

Take a look at the map on page 22. Track the path of this plague from southern Maine down to Narragansett Bay. It is a huge stretch of territory!

It is hard to fathom human devastation of this magnitude, so let's do some math to create a clearer picture. Using an 80 percent death rate figure (it's on the lower to middle side of the estimation), what is 80 percent of 70,000? That is 56,000 people.

Yes. That's right. 56,000 people. And that's just Wampanoag people, not the others north of us.

Continuing with the math: If 56,000 people died in a 2-year period, that means that 2,333 people died each month, 583 died each week, and about 83 people every day perished from this disease. And if 83 people a day die, how long for an entire village of 1,000 to succumb? That works out to 12 days. Not even 2 weeks. This plague was so overwhelming that people died within a couple of days of becoming ill. It was described as going through the country like "wildfire" because such great numbers of people perished so quickly within a short period of time. There was no one to take care of the sick or bury the dead. Indigenous people did not have immunity to these European diseases.

It is hard to imagine how Wampanoag and other tribal people felt going through this. Nothing the medicine people did, for all their knowledge, stopped this plague. No prayers or ceremonies, no herbs or medicines halted its rampage. These things had worked from time immemorial. Always. Until now. The sachems and other leaders could do nothing to stop it, either. No plans or decisions of the chiefs, clan mothers, elders, or warriors could stop it. People could only watch as entire villages, in many cases, got sick and died, with no one left at all.

The Pilgrims would not have been able to settle in "Plimoth" had it not been for the Great Dying. If all those Wampanoag people had not died, there would not have been room for the establishment of Plimoth

The epidemic, now called the Great Dying, killed tens of thousands of Wampanoag people, as well as others in the areas that it struck.

Colony. Massachusetts Bay Colony was established in 1630 in what is now the Boston area. This colony may also have never been established, at least at that time, if the plague had not happened. How would American history have been affected?

LET'S THINK ABOUT THIS:

1. Why would European ship captains think it was all right to kidnap Indigenous men? (Please refer back to the Doctrine of Discovery.)

2. What made the English believe Epenow's claim that there was gold on Capawack?

3. Think about the number of people who died in the plague. How many people live in your town or city? What would it look like if 80 percent of the people died? How would families be affected? How would businesses be affected? How would schools be affected? How would your neighborhood be affected? How would community life be affected?

4. In "When Life Was Our Own," how would life have changed for Little Bird and all of her family and relatives if they had gone through the plague?

CHAPTER 5

WHEN LIFE WAS OUR OWN: SUMMER'S ENDLESS DAYS

BERRY MONTH AND CORN MOUND HILLING

Summer wasted no time, as always, moving through its season. The corn was already knee-high, and the kids had done great work keeping all the corn thieves out of the fields! There had been much yelling at crows and blackbirds and chasing geese back down to the river. A small flock of geese could level a cornfield in a night if you weren't watchful. The men continued the nightly work of keeping the deer away. The cornstalks, showing bright green and dark red, were healthy and strong. The beans climbed them happily with their abundant red, white, or pink flowers, and the golden blossoms of squashes, pumpkins, and melons left no empty space as they emerged brightly among their own wide leaves.

These plants helped the men keep the deer and raccoons out as their long trailing vines were covered in scratchy prickles. Very irritating to tender raccoon paws and dainty deer ankles! The work of protecting the fields went on throughout the summer. Everyone saw lots of deer tracks, and those of many other animals, on all the pathways around the planting areas.

The time of season was here to trim other plants from growing between the mounds. Hoes for this were made from the shoulder blade bones of deer and elk. Strawberry figured a deer shoulder blade was about as big as her Dad's. He had made her a hoe this year so she could begin to help in the garden. Elk shoulder blades were about four times as big as Dad's or a deer's. Strawberry had never seen an elk. They mostly lived farther north but would sometimes travel this far south. Strong Bear loved elk meat and would always invite the wandering relative home for dinner!

As everyone had done in spring, families helped each other, going from field to field to scrape the weeds off at the surface of the ground. More earth was also piled on the mounds, care taken not to cover the bean and squash plants. Hilling the corn at this time gave extra support to the growing stalks, especially now that the bean plants were using them as poles.

Little Bird loved this time of the season—the beautiful colors in the fields, the sound of corn leaves rustling in summer breezes. She paused in her hoeing and held her face up to the sunlight, enjoying the cool wind blowing through. Strawberry, Punkinseed, and Woodchuck delighted in walking through the fields, seeing the corn husks forming and becoming fuller as the ears developed, and seeing the golden blossoms of squash, pumpkin, and melon wither as the fruit began to form. They checked on the progress of the beans every day—some were ripe and ready to be picked!

This was also the time of year that many other berries came into season. There were raspberries, blackberries, blueberries, and huckleberries. Little Bird and Strawberry went out daily with Grandma Yellow Sky to all the places where the berry relatives grew. The girls were getting quite skilled at knowing the land and where everything lived. Yellow Sky had them lead her to the blueberry and huckleberry fields, and the raspberry and blackberry patches. Just like with the strawberries, they always went by the first bushes. Just like with the strawberries, they said prayers of thanks and offered tobacco before they picked. And, just like with the strawberries, Strawberry's basket never seemed to get over half full! Little Bird reminded her of Mom's teasing when she had eaten too many. As Little Bird held her gaze on her sister, Strawberry blushed, her blackberry-filled hand stopping halfway to her mouth. She glanced at her Grandmother, who didn't need to say a word. She gave Strawberry "the look," and that was all that was needed. Strawberry put her handful of berries into her basket. She turned and went back to picking. She would not forget again.

Through the summer, the women and girls tended the cornfields, dug clams and quahogs, and gathered all the wild fruits and plants as they came into season. The men went fishing, in both fresh and salt water, depending on the type of fish to be caught and the time of the season.

Strong Bear, Tall Pine, and Walks in the Moonlight took the boys out eeling. Walks in the Moonlight had a boat that was more than big enough for all of them. Tall Pine sat in the rear to steer it, while Red Dawn sat in the front to paddle them forward. Strong Bear sat in the middle, between Woodchuck and River, to make sure they stayed intent on fishing and not swimming!

Each had a dip net made for their height, and their Uncle made sure they watched carefully for the slippery swimmers.

SUMMER DAYS, SUMMER NIGHTS

The hot days and bright blue skies of summer seemed endless. There were certainly plenty of rainy days, making the corn and all growing things seem so much taller than the day before. The sunflowers had reached the same height as Tall Pine, the tallest man in the family.

Not only were the green beans ripening but all the summer squashes as well. They were eaten fresh and not saved for winter, becoming delicious meals. Most of the beans were left right on the vines to dry, harvested through the end of summer.

There were many days of fishing, shellfishing, swimming, fires on the beach, and cooking. All the kids helped their families around their homes and cornfields. They went out together to gather firewood, collecting the lower dead branches from the trees. They helped their Moms take the cedar floor mats outside to shake out all the dust and sand. The girls tended the cook fires and got water from the spring for drinking and cooking and cleaning. They still manned the corn watches, mostly at dawn and dusk now. Raccoons and squirrels were not fussy about what stage the corn was in. Woodchuck came upon a raccoon one day, washing his little paws in the stream. He was certain the furry bandit was staring into the cornfield and licking his lips!

All the cousins spent time walking along the beaches and marshes, through the woods, meadows, swamps, and bogs. One day, Little Bird and Strawberry, River and Punkinseed, and Red Dawn and Woodchuck were out on the salt marsh collecting mussels.

Strawberry and Punkinseed stopped to count all the different birds they saw: two kinds of gulls, three kinds of hawks, swans, several types of little songbirds, four types of ducks, and one noisy blue jay. They heard crows off in the woods and figured they were near their rookery, since they were having quite the excited conversation!

They followed deer trails through the woods, and Red Dawn taught them to read tracks and the stories they told. You can tell if a deer is male or female, how much he weighs, whether he is happy and relaxed, just sauntering along, or whether he is hurrying or scared. So much to learn! He showed the kids other signs that tell you deer are around. They have the kind of teeth that shred branches, twigs, and grasses when they bite them off. Red Dawn was already skilled at this. Last winter he had gone out hunting for the first time with his Dad and Uncles. He tracked and found the first deer that they had killed. It was very humbling to hunt such a being and come face to face with its death. Now it really came home to him why only the animals needed are killed, and that everything from those animals is used and nothing wasted. He understood why there is much ceremony and thanksgiving offered when lives are to be taken.

The kids saw sign of all kinds of animals. They saw rabbit tracks and scat, or poop—a definite sign of animal presence! They saw little branches and grasses bitten clean off, telling what rabbits had for dinner. They tracked squirrels, raccoons, chipmunks, crows, otters, snakes, seagulls, hawks, spiders, beetles, turkeys, snails, geese, and bears. They carefully parted tall grasses in the fields and saw little mice and mole pathways. They went among the reeds along the riverbanks, to collect duck or goose eggs. They saw swan nests along the rivers, ponds, and swamps, but watched their graceful swimming from a distance. If swans think they or their babies are in danger, they might attack, and their wings are strong enough to break a bone!

They found woodchuck dens and otter slides into the river. They spent most of one afternoon watching a family of otters slide down a muddy bank into the water, run back up, and do it all over again. The otters were very funny together, and the kids covered their mouths as they laughed, so they would not scare these river comedians! They oohed and aahed when they saw downy, fuzzy goslings, ducklings, and cygnets following their parents around or hitching a ride on their backs.

There were many nights when Strong Bear took Little Bird and Strawberry out into the fields. They sat very still and quietly, hoping the fireflies might land on their open hands. They lay on their backs among the grasses and flowers, looking up at the night sky. Dad told the girls the history of the people and where we came from in the beginning. Strawberry already knew all the names of the stars, and how they moved in the sky as the seasons moved the earth. From where they sat on the hill, they could see the entire bay. One of Little Bird's favorite things was the way the moonlight made a sparkling path across the water. When it was a full moon night, it was almost like daylight outside.

And there were many nights that Grandpa Singing Wolf or Walks in the Moonlight took all the cousins out into the woods. They learned how to find their way in the dark and walk silently through the forest. The men had each of the kids find a special place in the woods. They had to be able to find their place in the dark, and then sit quietly, listening to the night sounds. Singing Wolf and Walks in the Moonlight taught the children to identify the creatures that moved about or flew at night. They learned their cries and calls, the sounds they make going about their night business. With this knowledge, the children learned not to be fearful but to be sure of themselves in the world. These are lessons everyone learns in their own time. At the moment, Strawberry and Punkinseed were quite sure they should learn these lessons together!

Little Bird found the perfect spot at the edge of the cedar swamp. There were three huge trees growing close together, with a triangle of earth built up between them. It was higher than the rest of the ground in the swamp, and dry. Heading for these trees, Little Bird always focused on moving silently, her feet carefully feeling the ground so she wouldn't snap a twig. One night as she sat, she heard a sudden, piercing, little scream right behind her at the edge of the forest. She jumped to her feet, her heart pounding in her chest. She could just barely make out the shape of a huge owl, lifting back into the night sky. He made absolutely no sound as he flew. Judging from the screech, Little Bird thought the owl had gotten himself a rabbit dinner.

Bear and Tall Pine's father, usually walked with the kids through the woods. As elders, they knew more about the history of the people and the ways of the forest and the earth. The kids loved spending time with them, listening to them speak of history, humor, and ancient teachings that endlessly flowed from generation to generation. They and the land carry many stories!

It was the height of summer, and the clan mothers announced it was time for Green Bean Ceremony. The many types of beans planted all started as green beans, the first vegetable to be ready for harvest. Again, as at strawberry time, the families gathered for ceremony and prayer, singing and dancing, thanking the beans for all they gave the people. And again, there was much cooking and feasting, people bringing baskets of fresh green beans, field greens, fish, shellfish, and turkeys.

After all the feasting, dancing, singing, and cleanup, the cousins ended up at Smiling Dove and Strong Bear's house. Everybody was pretty tired and couldn't wait to lie down to sleep. The fire in the house had been tamped down, so it would remain cool on such a hot night, and Yellow Sky and Singing Wolf were already sound asleep in their bed.

Smiling Dove was also lying down inside the

house, sinking into the soft furs that covered the bed.
Strong Bear and Walks in the Moonlight took turns
walking around their cornfields and resting by the
outdoor fire. All six cousins wanted to sleep outdoors
under the stars on bulrush mats around the fire. Little
Bird, Red Dawn, River, and Woodchuck were asleep
before their heads hit the mats. Before very long,
though, they were roused by low rumbling, scuffling
sounds that penetrated their sleep. Red Dawn raised
his head just enough to see his two littlest cousins,
Strawberry and Punkinseed, giggling and whispering
and rolling around. *How* could they still be awake?
There's another Strawberry mystery! Walks in the
Moonlight was just about to fall into a de-e-ep sleep
when his eyes flew open as a peal of laughter jolted
him awake. Getting up, he picked up both girls—quite
an accomplishment between the wiggles and the gig-
gles! He loaded them into a canoe with some furs to
lie on and pushed off from the shore. Walks in the
Moonlight paddled down the river, the water rhyth-
mically splashing against the boat. The girls began to
quiet down as they saw yellow eyes peer at them from
the woods on the riverbank. An owl hooted a greeting as they went by, and deer looked up from drinking
at the water's edge. An occasional bullfrog croaked
over a chorus of other singing frogs and crickets. A

light heron rose from the shore, gliding into the midnight blue. The sky had at least a million stars. Strawberry and Punkinseed lay contentedly on their backs,
trying to count them. They got all the way to nineteen
before both girls were breathing heavily and sound
asleep. Walks in the Moonlight also breathed—a sigh
of relief as he turned the boat to head back home.

THE CEDAR TREES SHARE

Grandma Yellow Sky gathered her two granddaughters and had them get some of the cedar bark
from the saplings cut earlier for house frame poles.
The bark had been rolled into coils and dried, saved
for future projects. Yellow Sky thought it was time
for the girls to learn to weave cedar bark mats. Used
on the floors, these mats kept bugs from wandering
in, as they don't like the strong smell of cedar. Strawberry thought that sounded good, preferring that
crawly things lived in their own houses.

The cedar bark turned a warm shade of brown
when it dried, and the girls wanted to add some other
colors to their mats. They decided to dye some of the
bark red and black to weave different patterns with.
Grandma Yellow Sky helped them bring the large clay

pots for dyeing over to the outdoor kitchen. Placing them on their stone tripods, Grandma had the girls fil them halfway with water.

Strawberry really wanted to learn how to build a fire—she was, after all, six now. So under Grandma's watchful eye, Little Bird had her sister get some dried outer bark of the cedar and make little piles under each pot. Then she had Strawberry gather a baske full of twigs and small branches and place them in crisscross layers over the shreddy cedar bark. Next she very carefully had her put one end of a long stick in the main cook fire. When the stick had a steady flame burning, Strawberry, being so cautious she moved in slow motion, put the burning end into the shredded cedar bark under each pot. The cedar and twigs burs into flame immediately. Strawberry sat back, relieved that her first fire making went so smoothly! Little Bird reminded her that she must now watch the fire, add ing more twigs as needed. She had to keep it burning steadily to heat the water and keep it boiling while the bark was being dyed.

Before long, the water began to bubble. Little Bird had brought out baskets of black walnut hulls for black dye, and madder root and some of the cedar bark for red. Strawberry placed several handfuls of each into the boiling water. They let the dye stuff boil for a while to release its colors into the water. Then Grandma and Little Bird helped Strawberry put several coils of the dried cedar bark into each pot. The bark would need to "cook" in the dye bath for the rest of the morning. Even if it wasn't being dyed, the bark would have to soak to become pliable enough to split it into strips for weaving without breaking it.

Little Bird went to collect more twigs, while Strawberry eagerly practiced her newfound skill of keeping the little fires at the right heat. She noticed a tiny bug heading for the flames and shooed him off in another direction. Another day for him—or her? she couldn't tell yet—to live and do his bug work.

While they waited, Grandma had them check a large bag of basswood bark cordage stored under the bed. Like the cedar, this inner bark was also collected in spring. Basswood was very different from cedar, though. Instead of being one smooth sheet, it grew in thin, wispy layers. It reminded Little Bird of dried leaves in the fall. Except thinner. And longer.

When two strands of basswood bark were twisted together, the cordage was very strong. People made both seine and dip nets for fishing, snare roping for animal traps, and cordage for weaving the edges of the cedar bark mats such as the girls were planning. The bag had plenty of newly made cordage for the girls to begin their weaving. Grandma Yellow Sky helped them pick out the right size cord for the mat weaving. Some of it was very thin like string, and some had been made into thick rope. It just depended on what it would be used for.

All the dyeing and digging through cordage had given Strawberry quite an appetite! Little Bird also felt more than a little hungry with the morning's work. Smiling Dove had been preparing food under the cooking arbor while the girls worked. Strong Bear had brought home four ducks from an early morning hunt. Mom had plucked, gutted, and cleaned the birds, and had them roasting on a spit over the fire. They were almost done, with such a tantalizing aroma! Strawberry's mouth watered as she watched them brown over the fire. Mom had a pot of corn soup going with some wild onion, garlic, and the last of the dried cranberries from last fall's harvest.

The girls got Grandma's and Grandpa's bowls and spoons, as well as their own, and waited in stomach-growling anticipation. When everything was done, they brought Yellow Sky and Singing Wolf their dinner. Smiling Dove filled a bowl for Strong Bear, gave each of the girls meat and soup, then took some for herself. Singing Wolf offered the prayer of thanksgiving before everyone started to eat. Strawberry decided she really loved roast duck as she crunched the crispy skin!

After they ate, Little Bird and Strawberry checked their dye pots. The cedar bark had been simmering for most of the morning, and Yellow Sky told the girls they could let the fires die out. She instructed them to leave the bark in the water until it had time to cool.

Later, all the cousins helped Little Bird and Strawberry take the cedar bark out of the dye baths. They hung the coils to dry on branch pegs on the support poles of the cook arbor, under its new roof of ash bark. The dye pots had cooled enough to empty, but they were too heavy to lift with the water still in them. The kids took turns with old elm bark buckets to scoop the water out and dump it near the shell heap. This turned into a race, with Strawberry, Punkinseed, and Woodchuck laughing in delight at the game. More dye water got spilled on the way to the shell heap than actually made it there—mostly on clothes, legs, and feet. Good thing the cedar bark absorbed most of the color, or the kids would have colorful clothes and toes for a while!

SUMMER STORMS

The girls headed out to the beach. One of their favorite places was a creek that flowed up into a salt marsh. Swimming in salt water was different than in fresh—it was easier to float, and the current would carry you when the tide was coming in. At low tide the creek was not deep enough for them to swim in, but they would explore along the marsh flats. There were countless little crabs that had one claw much larger than the other. They scuttled across the flats and disappeared down into little holes in the marsh before you could get close! If you waited quietly and didn't move, they would begin to peer out at you, thinking—hoping—you had left, ducking back to safety when they saw you.

Little Bird and Strawberry walked back to the shore and sat on the warm sand, digging their toes into the soothing heat. Down the beach, their cousins came walking toward them. River was eleven and almost as old as Little Bird. His little sister Punkinseed was the same age as Strawberry. Woodchuck was ten, and Red Dawn, at fourteen, was the oldest.

Everyone jumped into the ocean, swimming and splashing and diving. Red Dawn did a handstand, while Strawberry and Punkinseed dove underwater to inspect this feat they were still too short to try! Everyone began counting all the horseshoe crabs. Singing Wolf had told them many stories—how long these ancient beings have lived on Turtle Island (North America). Woodchuck remembered Grandpa telling them the history of Creator making the world on Turtle's back. He wondered if Horseshoe Crab lived then. On the way home, the kids each picked up two large horseshoe crab shells. They could stitch them together to make baskets and save the tails for fishing spears.

The wind was picking up, and huge dark clouds crowded over the horizon. The cousins could hear thunder rumbling in the distance. Rain was on its way, hopefully not so heavy that it would beat down the corn plants but give them enough water to keep growing. The storm wind brought a chill as the rain began, and they hurried back to Little Bird and Strawberry's house. The sky opened up before they made it back and soaked them to the bone! Grandma Yellow Sky greeted them with hot tea made from fresh-picked mint. The cousins changed into dry clothes and sat together around the fire. The heat of the flames was warm and comforting, and with the tea, the goose bumps on their arms began to fade away.

The thunder and lightning went on awhile. Lying on the end of the bed, Little Bird had a bird's-eye view out the door of the house. She loved the thunder and lightning, the wind and the rain. She watched the huge dark storm clouds forming and rolling, scudding across the sky in the wind. Strawberry and Punkin seed sat behind her, playing with their dolls. The boys were at the other end of the bed, talking quietly with Grandma and Grandpa. Somehow the storm made you feel like you should whisper. . . .

After a time, the storm began to lessen. The dark clouds rushed away, and the sun came out just in time to begin setting. The kids ventured outside, stepping into the heat of the last rays of sunshine setting on their shoulders. It made the newly washed land bright and crisp and fresh.

Smiling Dove made a stew for dinner from the leftover duck meat. Yellow Sky had collected fresh onions and garlic and some milkweed greens before it started raining. As milkweed sprouted through the soil, people collected the top two tiny, newest leaves. Not from all the plants but from half of them. Yellow Sky offered prayers of thanksgiving before picking and gathered enough tender leaves for dinner. All the cousins had a good meal, thanking their Aunt before heading home.

A MAN'S WORK NEVER ENDS

Strong Bear, Tall Pine, and Walks in the Moonlight went fishing together just about every day. They would round up all the boys, Red Dawn, River, and Woodchuck, making sure they had all their fishing equipment in good repair and ready to go. Tidal nets were hung and checked for holes or tears. Basswood or cedar bark fiber was rolled into line. All the boys had been making their own fishline for several years now. They worked with bone, antler, or wood to make many different types of fishhooks. Only Red Dawn had worked making copper hooks. That was a whole different skill compared to shaping the other materials. They hafted their collection of horse-shoe crab tails onto long handles with basswood or hickory bark fiber and hide glue, making spears for flounder and other fish. This year they had only one good trap left for catching eels, so both their Grand-pas, Singing Wolf and Rabbit, helped them collect tall slender saplings to construct new traps. The fish or eels swam into a wide opening that gradually narrowed, and the fish could not figure out how to escape. The boys checked the dip nets that might need repair after the spring's herring and salmon

runs. Red Dawn helped Woodchuck and River ma[...]
a new frame for one that was completely broke[...]
When it was finished, they took turns making th[...]
new netting.

As every fishing trip began, everyone gathered t[...]
offer tobacco and thanksgiving. Any life, all life the[...]
Creator made, was sacred and belonged only to itself[...]
Their prayers acknowledged the sacrifice of the fis[...]
and humbly thanked them for their gift. They fishe[...]
in the rivers, lakes, ponds, and the ocean, depend[...]
ing on the kind of fish and the season. Woodchuck[...]
especially loved taking the canoes out into the ocea[...]
to catch bluefish or cod or striped bass. He worke[...]
hard to handle the boat as smoothly as Tall Pine, wit[...]
all his experience maneuvering through currents anc[...]
large waves. They paddled out a ways, his Uncle[...]
and cousins in boats nearby, using hooks and line anc[...]
sometimes dip nets. Woodchuck practiced using th[...]
paddle to keep the boat steady against the pull of th[...]
current.

On other days, at high tide, they took the larg[...]
tidal nets and secured them to standing posts tha[...]
had been placed in the water. When the tide wen[...]
out, a large catch of different fish was trapped in the[...]
net. The fish were shared between the families, anc[...]
what was not eaten fresh was smoked over the fire[...]

to save for winter meals. Freshwater also provided much abundance—trout, perch, rock bass, pickerel, and many other kinds of fish.

While all the Dads and boys spent their days fishing, Singing Wolf and Rabbit decided to make a new dugout canoe. The two elders went out to look for a tree that would make a four-man canoe. The tree had to be the right size and near the water, so when finished, it would not be such a difficult task getting it into the river. Even a small twenty-foot boat required twenty men to lift it, never mind carry it! Launching boats was accomplished by placing smooth logs underneath and rolling them into the water.

The men finally selected a white pine that was about a hundred feet tall and four feet in diameter. They held ceremony to acknowledge the tree giving up its life, and thanksgiving for that generosity. They understood this tree was part of a family who would respond to the loss of their relative. Such loss creates a disruption in the energy and spirit that balances life. Ceremony heals the disruption and maintains the balance.

This was an average-size tree that had a straight, even width almost thirty feet long in one section of the trunk. Yellow Sky, Smiling Dove, and Little Bird gathered clay and brought it to the tree. (Grandpa

Rabbit's wife, who was Strong Bear and Tall Pine's mother, had passed away a few years ago, or she would have joined the women in the clay gathering. The men packed a nice thick ring of clay around the trunk about hip high up from the ground. Next, they built a fire around the entire base of the tree. The clay would prevent the fire from burning farther up the trunk, potentially marring the part that would become the boat. Singing Wolf and Rabbit didn't need a huge roaring fire for this job, just a low steady one. As the fire burned around the tree, the men used stone-bladed axes to chop away the charred wood.

Burning and chopping a tree this size until it fell took almost two days. During the night, the men took turns, sleeping awhile or watching the fire and scraping away the charred wood. The women had brought a clay kettle, and nocake, dry corn, and beans. In the morning, Grandpa Rabbit got the cook fire going and started some soup. As the food simmered, he went to the river and caught three trout. Grandpa cleaned them and hung them from spits to roast, once the corn and beans were just about done. The fish would not take long to cook. He stirred some nocake meal into the soup to thicken and flavor their breakfast.

By the following morning, the tree was ready to fall. Its immense weight shook the earth when it hit the ground, and people felt the tremors all the way back in the cornfields. The two men took a moment to acknowledge what they were receiving from this giant being whose life had just passed. To honor that life, every part of that tree, every branch and twig, would be used.

The next job was to cut the straight section from the rest of the trunk. This was also done with fire, the main woodworking tool. The burned, charred wood was softer and much easier to scrape away than chopping green wood. Singing Wolf and Rabbit had showed Strong Bear and Tall Pine, when they were boys, how to use fire with maple, oak, hickory, walnut, or cherry burls to create bowls and cups, spoons, and ladles and stirring paddles, whether for eating a small cup of soup or serving a large roasted turkey.

And as they had learned, they now taught their boys Red Dawn, River, and Woodchuck the skill of carefully tending embers to burn in the right spots, scraping away the char to create the desired utensil. As they became skilled carvers, they adorned each utensil so that bowls had duck heads or bears at either end, and spoons and ladles had hawks, turtles, or deer emerging from the handles. Last year, Red Dawn had made his mother a new serving bowl from a very large maple burl. When the burl was separated from the tree, a sizable piece of the trunk came off with it. In that wood Red Dawn saw a graceful swan, which he carved to float on the edge of the bowl. Stands Strong was so pleased with her beautiful gift! Her son also made her a new mortar from a three-foot section of oak log, burning it down halfway to create enough depth for grinding corn.

Woodchuck was just starting his third spoon. He was finally understanding how to burn just enough of the little burl to make the spoon even and smooth. He was too eager with his first spoon, working too fast with the fire. He completely burned away the bowl of the spoon from its handle! On his second try, he was better at controlling the process of blowing through a hollow reed, conducting air and fanning the embers to burn in the desired spots. Woodchuck thought he was finally accomplishing this skill! Until he noticed he could see the ground right through that new hole in the bottom of his spoon! Tall Pine and Rabbit had to smile and commend Woodchuck on his enthusiasm for learning. Woodchuck, however, couldn't hide his disappointment at creating another piece of firewood. Grandpa Rabbit said another day, another lesson, a new small burl to begin again.

Tall Pine, Strong Bear, and Walks in the Moonlight began making plans to travel to the soapstone quarry. They needed the stone to make pipes for smoking and ceremony. This coming winter, Red Dawn would go out on his own for a number of weeks. He would test his skills on building shelter, getting food and water, and making fire to keep warm and cook. He would need a pipe to smoke and pray with. The men also made small bowls for mixing paints or other such jobs, and beads for necklaces and jewelry. Some people still had large bowls or cooking kettles that ancestors had made from the soapstone, long before they made clay kettles. The quarry was almost an entire day's walk away. The men would collect as much stone as they could, enough to make all the things they would need until they could return the following year.

As always, they did not go into the quarry and just start breaking off rock. They offered tobacco and prayed, asking permission to use these bones of Mother Earth, to help them fulfill their needs.

The men and boys worked with many different types of stone to make all the tools and weapons that they used. Knowledge and skill were passed down through generations, children learning from elders, watching them closely, to not miss any detail of method or technique. They were guided and encouraged, and by the time they were Red Dawn's age, they had the ability to make all the dishes, utensils, tools, and equipment they would ever need.

Soapstone was used for certain things because it

is softer and easier to work with than harder stone. I was carved into pipes, easily drilled through to make small beads, or shaped into round flywheels for pump drills. Harder stone was shaped by different methods to make a wide variety of tools. White quartz, dark cherts, and felsites were knapped into arrowpoints of many different sizes, depending on what would be hunted—an elk, a turkey, or a pigeon. Men used these ancient technologies to make spearpoints, knife blades, pestles, hammer stones, and ax blades. They made adzes for woodworking projects such as making canoes, small stone mortars and pestles for grinding paints, and fish net weights. They incorporated the natural design within different stone into their finished works. The older men produced so many pieces that revealed not only great beauty but also their lifelong experience. Red Dawn was now quite skilled at knapping arrowheads or pecking (hitting the soon-to-be tool with another rock to shape it) an ax head. Yet even he, and all the younger boys, watched in amazement as their Grandfathers knapped arrowheads or knife blades as easily as slicing through boiled bread. Grandpa Rabbit once made six arrowpoints from early morning to midday. They marveled at how easily he broke rock into pieces to shape into different tools. On one of River's early attempts, he broke a rock into several pieces cleanly, only to cut his thumb badly on a razor-sharp sliver. Grandma Yellow Sky went to the spiders for help, left a pinch of tobacco, and gathered a good amount of web to pack the cut and stop the bleeding.

Red Dawn had been working hard, preparing for his winter quest. He had made an ash wood bow, a number of arrows, including the wooden shafts, stone or bone points, and some of copper, and fletching them with sections cut from turkey wing feathers. He knew the bow worked, because since he had made his Mom the big serving bowl, he figured he might as well fill it with a turkey to roast. A bit taller than himself, his bow was strong and true.

GATHERING WITH GRANDMA: PLANTS AS ELDERS, PLANTS AS TEACHERS

The next day Grandma Yellow Sky and the girls walked through the woods to check on all the different plants they used for food or medicine, cordage, baskets, and weaving. They checked on all the plants regularly to see if they were ready for harvest, if they needed to be thinned or otherwise tended to make them flourish. They went to all the familiar places, not visited since last summer. The wild onion and garlic grew prolifically in early summer, and Smiling Dove added some to the cook pot every day. She also dried some, picking the stalks while they were small and tender. Even by the time the yellow squash began to ripen, they became tough and inedible. They went to where the raspberries, blackberries, and blueberries all grew. The rasps and blacks were in flower, but it was still early for the blues. The elderberries had only very new berry buds, fruiting after the blueberries, just before harvest time.

They saw so many grapevines and collected some of the small new leaves. In spring and early summer, they made a nice green vegetable in soups. Later on, when the leaves grew large, they were used to wrap corn cake dough in, to place in the ashes of the fire to bake. Then in the fall, of course, were the grapes themselves! You could walk down the path and inhale their inviting scent as it laced the air, hinting of good things to come. When the vines dried, they would be collected and stored for making baskets.

Grandma had such a vast knowledge of everything in the forest. She knew what plants to check on when, where they grew, and how to pick and store them. She knew how to make all kinds of teas, tinctures, salves, and poultices—all kinds of medicines for all kinds of sickness or injury. Just looking around at all the different plants in the woods, the fields, the marshes and beaches, and the swamps and bogs gave the girls an understanding of the depth of her knowledge. Strawberry often felt like her head was spinning as she listened to her Grandma speak about the plants, and how she spoke to them when she offered tobacco. Would she ever remember all this? Would she ever even learn to make a tea like Grandma did to wash her knee when she fell and scraped it? Well, she was only six, so she figured she probably had some time yet to learn about the plants. Little Bird especially loved hearing Grandma's stories of learning from her own Grandma, who had learned from hers, who had learned from hers.

All the kids were showed how to walk through the woods and fields, being aware of where they placed their feet, so they didn't trample and crush any plants or grass or bugs or other small relatives.

They walked along the rivers and freshwater swamps, checking on both the bulrush reeds and the wide leaf cattail. These were both used to make the mats for house coverings. They checked the natural springs where watercress grows.

They walked through the forests, checking on ferns, sumac, wood lily, jack-in-the-pulpit, grapevines, elderberry, blackberry, raspberry, and blueberry bushes. They walked through vast fields of grasses and milkweed, dogbane, violets, yellow dock, and burdock. Little Bird felt like she was doing really well at remembering all that Yellow Sky was telling them about each of the plants and the places where they grew.

Grandma taught them to remain aware and observe how the plants grew and matured over the spring and summer. They learned to see when the plant, or any of the various parts, would be ready to harvest. Grandma had helped them each make a small deerskin pouch to carry tobacco. They wore these around their necks and were ready to offer thanksgiving every time they went out to gather. Yellow Sky instructed them in collecting the plants in a respectful manner, understanding that the plants were giving up their lives so we can eat and have medicine, and make baskets and nets and other things we need.

They walked the beaches with Grandma to check on the height of the beach grass, used for weaving baskets. It was a very hot day, but a cooling breeze came off the water that smelled refreshingly of salt air. They came to a spot where there were a number of big rocks on the shore and sat to rest for a while

Strawberry and Little Bird sat very still with their feet in the water, watching minnows come up and nibble at their toes. They found horseshoe crab shells, and Grandma helped them bind two together to make baskets. She always carried her sewing pouch with her, tied to her belt. You never know when you'll need an awl or a sharp cutting edge or some string or leather or rawhide strips. She showed Little Bird how to carefully make a row of holes with the awl along the edges of the shells. Grandma wasn't totally convinced that Strawberry was ready to handle an awl. The shells are fairly fragile and would break with too much pressure. Plus, the holes should be in the shell, and not

Little Bird loved to watch her Grandma's hands as she wove so many different plant materials into so many baskets!

in the fingers! Once Little Bird had completed this, Grandma handed her some basswood bark string to poke through the holes to tie the shells together. The last thing was to add a length of leather strip for handles. Now each of them had a new basket!

They were coming to a salt marsh and planned to dig some mussels and quahogs to take back for dinner. Strawberry, for her part, missed that segment of the conversation! She was walking along the high tide mark, where the waves had washed up eel grass which stretched down the beach for a very long way. There were all sorts of treasures hidden in the piles of seaweed. There were orange and yellow jingle shells, slipper shells, skate's egg sacs—never now to become a skate—many beautiful and interesting rocks and pebbles of different colors, sizes, and textures. She even found a whole baby quahog shell that had some purple along the inner edge. She supposed that a hungry crab or starfish had pried open the shell and helped himself to such a tender morsel. That thought tugged at Strawberry's heart because she felt very strongly when something had to die.

She made herself think of what Mom and Dad, and Grandpa and Grandma, had always told her. Crabs and starfish have to eat to live. It is all part of Creator's plan, and everything on the earth is part of that plan. It's a really good plan, when you think about it! Creator made all sorts of living things, like everything in Creation—all the animals, plants, stars, winds, waters, mud, clay, cranberry bogs, clouds, bugs—just everything. Everything in Creation was given a job. And as long as everybody does their job, the balance of the world will be kept. Creation will work like it is supposed to. People were to make sure that Creator's plan for life was kept working as created. So when people have to take the lives of animals or plants to eat or make things they need, that is acknowledged and thanksgiving offered. Also, in taking for our needs, we have to make sure that those beings have all they need to live their lives. It still gave Strawberry a pit in her stomach when Dad or Uncle Tall Pine killed deer, but she understood that the deer died so that they could eat and live. And she liked deer meat! Her family also taught her that they burned the underbrush every spring and fall, as then the new growth of plants offered the deer food. Dad and Uncle Tall Pine also only hunted in winter and looked especially for the bucks, killing as quickly and mercifully as possible. They did not hunt in spring when the does were having their fawns. And this is the same reason that they walked by a whole patch of strawberries and went on to others.

GATHERING CLAY—FROM THE BODY OF MOTHER EARTH

Grandma Yellow Sky gathered all the women in the family one morning to make preparations to go and gather clay. They would walk up the river a ways to the place where it was found. She had her daughters Smiling Dove, Blue Heron, and their daughters Little Bird, Strawberry, and Punkinseed, as well as Tall Pine's wife, Stands Strong.

Grandma made sure everyone had digging sticks and paddles to loosen and separate chunks of clay from the riverbank, and baskets to carry it home in. Everyone also had their pouches of tobacco or cornmeal or cedar. Clay is a kind of earth that forms the body of Mother Earth, and is one of the oldest ancestors. And like every other living being, when asked to give of herself, prayer and sacred tobacco were offered. It never entered anyone's mind to just go and thrust in a digging stick, disturbing Mother Earth without proper thanksgiving.

Little Bird already had her tobacco pouch. Strong Bear had showed her how to make it a few years ago and instructed her on handling the sacred plants like tobacco, cornmeal, cedar, sweetgrass, and sage.

Now she helped Strawberry and Punkinseed each make their own pouch. Grandma Yellow Sky made sure everyone had tobacco. Each of the girls carefully plucked some small handfuls from Yellow Sky's bag and placed them in their own pouches, making certain not to drop one tiny piece on the ground.

The distance to the clay was about as far as from the winter villages to the summer homes. Once there, they laid down their baskets and digging tools and, holding hands in a circle, offered their prayers. Only then did they dig into the riverbank for clay. It didn't take very long at all for everyone to fill their baskets. Strawberry watched her sister and her Mom and Grandma as they tied their tumplines, or carrying straps, to either side of their baskets, and she did the same. The straps each had a wide section that was placed across the chest, so that the baskets were carried at their backs. The clay-filled baskets, while not huge, were still pretty heavy. So, rather than lift the baskets and swing them around to their backs, they were left on the ground, and the women stepped into the tumplines, lifting the baskets with the straps in place. This was the easiest way to manage the weight, considering they still had to walk home.

Little Bird and the older women made it look so easy! In one smooth move, their tumplines were in place with baskets behind. Everyone waited while Strawberry and Punkinseed tried to emulate their graceful moves. The little girls' baskets were much smaller, but Strawberry tipped hers and almost spilled the clay, while Punkinseed clotheslined herself until she figured out how to get the tumpline in the right position. This was the first clay trip for Strawberry and Punkinseed, who waddled like a couple of ducks for a while, before they got the rhythm of walking with the weight on their backs. And on the way home, they only had to stop three times to rest and drink some fresh water!

Little Bird kept an eye on her little sister and cousin. She could see them getting tired and starting to drag their feet! She prayed again—that the girls would make it home, and no one would have to carry them and their clay as well! But make it home they did. Everyone set their baskets just inside the door of Blue Heron's house. From that spot, it was about the length of a stirring paddle, two to three feet, to the bed with the nice, comfortable piles of furs. To Strawberry and Punkinseed, it looked more like the length of a cornfield! With a final burst of energy, they hoisted themselves onto the bed and were asleep before they hit the furs. Two little somebodies would be having a late supper tonight!

Now that the clay had been gathered, the real

work would begin! The next day the women came back to Blue Heron's house and brought it outside. They spread all the chunks onto old bulrush mats and broke up the larger ones into pieces no bigger than Strawberry's fist. The clay was left to dry in the sun, which still might take a few days even with good, hot sunny weather. Once dried, the chunks were then pounded into powder. This was done a ways from the house, as it created a lot of clay dust. Plus, you had to sit on the upwind side so that the dust wouldn't fill your nose, mouth, and lungs. And coat your skin, and get all in your hair and on and under your clothes. However, that didn't complete the dusty work! Once powdered, the clay had to be sifted to remove any little plant parts, twigs, or pebbles that had gotten embedded in it. These things would not allow the clay to be worked smooth and would cause a pot to break during the firing-hardening process.

Little Bird had done this work a few times now, and the clay dust always found its way under her belt! Like it aimed for just that spot, where the seemingly smooth, powdery clay would rub and feel gritty. Jumping in the river was the best way to get rid of the grit. Even if you vigorously shook your clothes, you could still raise a cloud of dust if you gave your leg a good slap when you put them back on.

Anyway, once the clay was dried and powdered,

it could be stored until pottery making was to begin. Smiling Dove and Blue Heron gathered the girls. They all joined Grandma Yellow Sky, who was sitting in the shade of the huge oak tree and beginning to build a clay pot. The girls watched as she mixed some powdered clay with water and kneaded it between her hands, working out all the air and making it smooth. When that was done, she made a shallow hole in the ground the size of the bottom of a medium-size kettle and laid a large scrap of deerskin in it. Taking her worked clay, she patted it into a thin disc and placed it into the hole, smoothing it to fit that shape. Then she formed more clay into "ropes" that were the length of the rim of the disc. She laid a clay rope on the rim and smoothed the two pieces together with her thumb. Grandma repeated this process over and over, building and shaping her new clay kettle.

Little Bird had scraped out a shallow hole to form her kettle bottom and was working a handful of clay for the disc. Strawberry was fascinated, watching Grandma Yellow Sky's hands at work. They moved smoothly, surely, and confidently—not what Strawberry was feeling at the moment. She had tried to make a pot before. The first time, the sides kept collapsing in as she added the ropes and tried to smooth them into a pot. The next time, she actually finished a small pot, but thought it looked more like a moon rock than a pot, kind of misshapen and lonely. Plus, it blew up during the firing process. But—she would try again. She so badly wanted to make pottery as easily as her Grandma did!

So she and Punkinseed scraped out holes for the pot bottoms, being very careful to make them even and absolutely round—not too deep and not too shallow—and laid in their pieces of deer hide. They each had powdered clay in a bowl, and gingerly added water. They didn't want to add too much, because then they would have to keep adding clay. And pretty soon, they might have enough for forty pots! Both girls felt that trying to make one pot today would be quite sufficient. So they added a little water and mixed, and added a little more and mixed, and pretty soon the clay was just right. They each took a little handful of clay (which was very convenient since they only had little hands) and began to form the discs for the kettle bottoms. They concentrated very hard on their work, trying not to make one side too thick and the other too thin. Punkinseed seemed to have a better knack than Strawberry, and even though it took her a while, she presently placed her disc on the deerskin and gently shaped it into the rounded bottom. Strawberry was so focused on her disc, she hadn't noticed that her cousin had finished this step of the process. She was finally able to lay the piece on her deerskin, but while it was an even thickness, it was too thin. It overflowed the hole, lying limply all around the edge.

While Punkinseed could now begin making ropes to build the body of her pot, Strawberry had to start over to get her kettle bottom the right thickness. She scooped up her disc, rolled it back into a ball, and again began pinching it out into a new one. Grandma Yellow Sky kept her eye on Strawberry's work but didn't offer any advice or commentary. She saw that Strawberry was figuring this out on her own and left her to that process. It didn't matter how long it took her—only that she learned. Getting that experience in her fingers was the best teacher.

Grandma Yellow Sky, Smiling Dove, and Blue Heron all completed their pots by midafternoon. Grandma's was quite large and round. It was not as big as a feast pot, but it would still cook enough food for her entire family to have seconds! The two Moms each finished medium-size kettles, such as were cooked in every day. Everyone always had spare kettles on hand. The women set their finished pots on three stones, just as they would in cooking. They would let them dry until the clay was firm enough to incise or draw designs in. Everything anyone made, whether a mat, a pot, basket, bow or arrows, or clothing, was always made beautiful with decoration—a reflection of the beauty the Creator gave us on the Earth.

Little Bird also finished her pot, smaller than those of the women but evenly round and smooth. It, too, would soon be ready for a design on its rim. Punkinseed was almost done with her pot. She just had to add the rim, before letting it dry enough to incise her design. Strawberry had kept steady and focused on her work, and she had completed the disc for the kettle bottom. This time it was just the right size, pretty even and smooth, and able to support the weight of the clay ropes. And the next rope, and the next one, and the next one. Her pot was halfway done, and while not as smooth and round as the others, it wasn't a lumpy moon rock, either! Finally, Strawberry thought, she was learning to make a clay pot! Her fingers started to feel like they knew what they were doing!

Once everyone had finished decorating their pots, there was one final step before they could be used for cooking. They needed to be fire-hardened, which made them stronger to last longer. But before they could be fired, they had to be completely dry. If there was any moisture left in the clay or any air bubbles, the heat of the firing would make the pots explode. So the newly created kettles sat on their tripods, out of everyone's path. There they would stay for half a month, only being moved indoors should it rain. The job of firing the pots would be the work of another day.

GREEN CORN TIME

It was now fully the height of summer. Hot sunny days mixing with just the right number of rainy days made the gardens full and lush. Baskets of beans were picked every day, with most left to mature and dry on the vine, ready for winter meals. The summer squashes produced abundantly, while the winter squashes were just starting to bud and grow. Golden squash and yellow melon flowers wilted as their fruit started

Giving thanks for Corn Mother and all Creator has given us.

to form. The sunflowers were even taller than Tall Pine. Heavy with new seeds, they nodded their heads on midsummer breezes. The corn had become Green Corn, the early milk stage before maturing into beautiful red, yellow, blue, and white kernels. This first corn of the season marked the beginning of harvest time.

Once again, the clan mothers gathered the families together, this time to plan for the Green Corn Ceremonies. They would remember how Crow brought corn to the people from Creator's garden, and how Corn Mother taught them to plant her with the beans and squashes, feeding the earth as they took their nourishment from her. The people sang thanksgiving to the Creator and caressed the earth with dancing.

After the ceremonies was a huge feast. All the Moms, Grandmas, and Aunties had so many different ways to cook and prepare green corn. Strawberry and Punkinseed managed to attend about four different family gatherings, making their way through the fields to celebrations of the different clans. Always warmly invited in, they got to try four different green corn recipes, which were sweet, tender, and delicious! Neither girl could decide which she liked best as they headed home, munching on ash cakes made with nocake and green corn kernels. Neither

Strawberry nor Punkinseed could remember from whom they received this delicious treat, but that lady was a really good cook! The cakes were moist and sweet, and melted in your mouth.

Mom had showed Strawberry how to mix the dough and add in just the right amount of berries or other ingredients. She had showed her how to collect large maple, burdock, or grape leaves to wrap her corn cakes in, and how to set them in the ashes of the fire. Not in the fire, but where the ashes were hot enough to cook the cakes. Strawberry was very confident that she knew all these steps now. After all, she was six! But she still had trouble figuring out how long to keep the cakes in the ashes. She worried if she didn't leave them in long enough, her family would be eating raw dough. If she left them in too long, they would be burnt and hard. Which is how her last batch turned out. Actually, the last three batches. Actually, in all fairness, the last batch was only very brown and the centers were soft. The others had been . . . way darker in color. Her family praised her efforts and her progress, eating the parts that could be eaten and letting the fire take the rest, along with the remains of the leaf wrappings.

So harvest was beginning, and summer was winding down. There was a lot of work to be done to make sure all the vegetables were gathered, dried, and put away for winter. While there were still plenty of long, hot days ahead, the light changes at this time of year and the air feels different—early hints of autumn.

SUMMER PASSING BY

Grandma Yellow Sky accompanied Smiling Dove, Blue Heron, Stands Strong, and all the girls to the river swamps to check the growth of the bulrush and cattail reeds. The river ran right through the middle of a huge swamp with a great patch of bulrush. Everyone was happy to see that they were tall and straight and healthy—and ready to be harvested!

The cattail reeds grew at another spot farther up the river. They, too, were ready for harvest. They were very tall—taller than Tall Pine, way taller actually, waving in endless succession as far as the eye could see. This section of swamp was usually dry ground, but getting to it required crossing a little stream. Depending on where the summer homes were, and what swamps they were near, the women sometimes had to gather both kinds of reeds by boat. Reaching them by water was easier than going through the swamp.

Walking through the reed fields was a skill to be learned indeed! The river "bottom" was the roots of the reeds and other plants growing together in a mesh, with open, cold, very deep—seemingly bottomless—water flowing underneath. You had to learn how to feel with your feet and walk on the strong parts of this root system. Should any given point in the root-mesh break through, your feet—and you—drop into the watery unknown!

The women made cattail mats for the outer coverings of the houses, usually the summer houses. In the winter villages, the men covered the homes with huge thick sheets of bark harvested in the spring. The cattails had natural qualities that helped the mats perform their basic function—to keep the rain and wind out. They did this by the shape of their leaves, the way they were sewn together, the thick sap contained in their leaves, and the fact that there were always at least two layers of mats at any given spot on the roof. New mats were made every year, for use the following summer. They were tied to the house frames, and last year's older mats were secured over them. That way the older ones got the brunt of the weather, which kept the newer mats in good shape for a second year.

The women also wove the bulrush mats, which lined the inside walls, providing insulation. With no fire inside, they kept the house cooler than outside in warmer months. In colder weather, they held the heat in, keeping the homes very warm.

Both types of mats were quite large. The bulrush could be as long as Strong Bear was tall, their width about half that much, up to his waist. The cattail mats were different lengths depending where on the house frame they would be placed. Little Bird already had experience making both types of mats, which really are projects for bigger people. Last year she set up the frame the mats are woven on next to an overturned boat. She wanted to show her sister how to weave bulrush mats. Strawberry was almost tall enough to reach the row being woven, but even so, her little hand could only hold two or three reeds at a time to do the weaving. Strawberry had grown like a well-watered sprout, so maybe bulrush weaving would be easier this year. Maybe she could grasp five or six reeds now. Little Bird had to admit that it is much easier to weave anything if you can reach it!

Little Bird and Strawberry discussed what colors and designs they would put into their mat. The reeds could be dyed different colors and all sorts of patterns woven in. When the houses were fully lined with the bulrush mats, they were very beautiful in addition to

As summer was clearly turning into fall, many things in the world became ready to harvest. Everyone was already saving corn husks, as the corn matured enough for picking. Grandma Yellow Sky took her granddaughters out to check and see if the beach grass was tall enough yet for basket weaving. They checked on the dogbane and milkweed, which were still too green. The milkweed seed pods were forming, another part of the plant eaten as a vegetable. For cordage fibers, the dogbane and milkweed were gathered later in the fall, when only the dried stalks remained and the leaves fallen off.

The beach plums were ripening now, both tart and sweet at the same time. They could be cooked into a pudding or added to boiled bread. The black cherries were fat and juicy on their branches, and people hurried to collect them. The birds loved them, too, but they didn't seem to grasp the concept of sharing! The cherry trees usually produce fruit only every other year.

And finally! Watermelon season was here! They were ripening nicely, as their smooth, round, dark green skins announced. Smiling Dove had already found four ready to be picked. When the girls came back from checking on the beach grass, dogbane, milkweed, and other plants, Mom had slices of juicy, sweet, pink melon waiting for them. The girls munched enthusiastically, quenching their thirst from their trek with Grandma. As they ate, they picked out the seeds and set them in a little bowl. Mom would later rinse and dry them to be stored for next year's planting. Strawberry tried really hard to keep the juice from running down her chin and down the front of her clothes. You know, like the strawberry juice? Mom had washed these clothes, but the big red strawberry splotch didn't come out. It was still visible. At least watermelon basically leaves water stains!

The men continued their daily fishing trips, bringing home many kinds of ocean fish and shellfish. Much of this was smoked and dried to keep for meals back in the winter village, when they were not near the ocean. In late summer, lots of seafood still went into daily recipes, whether a large fish was roasted over the fire or shellfish added to a soup or stew.

Strong Bear, Tall Pine, and Walks in the Moonlight met with several of the other men to plan a sturgeon fishing trip. Like the herring and the salmon, the sturgeon are born in fresh water, travel to the ocean to live their lives, and return to spawn in the same fresh water they were born in. They are just way bigger than their cousins!

The men set about getting their fishing gear

together, spears, rope, and torches. This would be a night expedition, just before the time the fish would come back to their freshwater birthplaces. The firelight of the torches attracted the sturgeon to the surface of the water where they could be speared. It was an amazing sight to see when all the boats were out, torches flaming and firelight reflecting off the water. Once killed, the fish were tied to the boat to be towed in. The sturgeon were much too large to be hauled into the boat. The men did not need to get a huge number of them, as a few would make meals for a lot of people. Once brought in to shore, they were cleaned and cut up, with some given to the sachems, the elders, and to everybody in the community.

CHAPTER 6

COLONIZATION: THE PRICE OF THE LAND

When asked to define the word "colony," people usually answer that a group of people leaves their country of origin, goes to another land, settles, makes their homes, and starts living there.

Is that all there is to the making of a colony, bringing colonization to another land?

Actually, that is only half the definition. The other half is what happens to the people who are already living in the "new" place when others come in.

Enormous changes happen—to the people, to their cultures, to the land itself. These changes take many forms and are designed to control, dominate, or even annihilate the original people. The *intent* of the newcomers is to obtain the land and the "resources" of the land, such as gold, timber, or furs, with the goal of creating wealth and profit.

The definition of "colonization" has to include the intent of those who are colonizing. What do they want? What are the reasons for coming to the new place? What are their goals? How will they accomplish their goals? What impact will all this have on the original people, their culture, the land itself? Does this impact matter?

Thinking more about these questions, what did the Pilgrims actually want? The popular history is that they came to America for religious freedom. Is that the whole story?

If the Pilgrims had remained in England, they could have been killed, as the king was enforcing his policy that everyone strictly follow the Church of England. The Pilgrims wanted to create changes to those teachings, taking their lives in their hands. They escaped England and went to Leiden in the Netherlands, a much more tolerant country. They spent twelve years there but became concerned their children would grow up to be culturally Dutch, and not English. They did not want this, so they arranged to come to America instead. Here, though they still considered themselves English citizens, they would be free to practice their religious beliefs without the fear of death.

Did they try to take over the Netherlands as their own country?

Colonization is not a single activity that happened once in the past and now, today, is over and done with. It is not the experience of a single individual or individuals but a multifaceted planned and purposeful *system* that utilizes multiple methods, processes, tools, and tactics to achieve its goals of wealth, profit, and control.

The following sections describe some methods of colonization, specifically those undertaken for America to become a country: the price of the land.

THE GREAT DYING AND OTHER FOREIGN DISEASES

Disease is one of the methods of colonization. Until the time of European contact, there were no known infectious diseases here. Indigenous people, therefore, had no immunity to them, and that was the reason tens of thousands died in a very short time.

The Great Dying is considered to have been introduced unintentionally. Nevertheless, as mentioned previously, it had a tremendously devastating impact on Wampanoag and several other Indigenous nations. This was very convenient for the Pilgrims when they arrived, to be able to settle here just two years later.

Let's take a closer look at the concept of the plague being "unintentional." Below is a quote from Captain John Smith taken from the writings he made on his voyages. He sailed along the coast of "New England" in 1614 and created some invaluable maps of the areas he traveled.

Smith wrote in his "Advertisements for the unexperienced planters of New England" about the Great Dying and the aftermath of it. This "advertisement" was designed to bring more English or European settlers to America in order to establish a colony.

Smith said, ". . . it seems God hath provided this Country for our Nation, destroying the natives by the plague, it not touching one Englishman . . . and as they [the Native people] report thus it began:

"A fishing ship being cast away upon the coast, two of the men escaped on shore; one of them died, the other lived among the natives till he had learned their language; then he perswaded them to become Christians, shewing them a Testament, some parts thereof expounding so well as he could, but they so much derided him, that he told them he feared his God would destroy them: whereat the King [the Chief of the Native people] assembled all his people about a hill,

himself with the Christian standing on the top, demanded if his God had so many people and able to kill all those?

"He answered yes, and surely would, and bring in strangers to possess their land: but not so long they mocked him and his God, that not long after such a sicknesse came, that of five or six hundred . . . there remained but thirty . . . : the two remaining fled the Country till the English came, then they returned and surrendered their Country and title to the English."

Let's think a little deeper about Smith's "advertisements." It is okay to question what is written and not just accept something as fact because it's on paper. It's critically important to learn to be a critical reader!

In regard to the two men who escaped from their ship, let's look at the word "escape." If this ship was here for the purpose of fishing, why would the two men need to escape? Would they rather stay with Indigenous people, whom they possibly considered savages, or get back home?

As for the man who died shortly after being left here, what did he die of? Were these two men actually the ones who brought the plague that killed tens of thousands of Indigenous people?

The second man lived with the Native people long enough to learn their language. That is a fair amount of time. Even if this man was not sick, he had contact with the man who died, possibly—possibly—from the plague. He could therefore have been a carrier of the disease, infecting the Indigenous people. Were they becoming ill while this man was learning their language?

The passage also says this man persuaded these Indigenous people to become Christians, but immediately contradicts that statement with the description of their reactions to his "persuasions."

The reactions of the English and other Europeans about the devastation of the plague are disturbingly revealing. Another Englishman, Nathaniel Morton, wrote a book called *New England's Memorial* in 1630. Like John Smith, Morton describes the French sailors who were left behind, the one who died right away and the other who "lived amongst them untill he was able to discourse with them, and told them,

"That god was angry with them for their wickedness, and would destroy them, and give their Country to another people, that should not live as beasts as they did, but should be clothed. . . . Shortly after his death came the plague, a Disease they never heard of before, and mightily swept them away, and left them as dung on the earth. . . ."

The "wickedness" that Morton refers to is the harsh treatment these French sailors received from the Indigenous people, who are stated to have "sent them from one Sachem to another to make sport of them, and used them worse than slaves."

I have to question why these Indigenous people would treat them this way. Native hospitality, as a way of building good relationships, is to be welcoming and tend to the needs of guests. Remember the Guanahaní who welcomed Columbus? It is still so in Indigenous cultures today. However, that concept has gone right out the window here, as Morton is stating it. Smith wrote about his observations before the plague struck (1614) and toward the end of its reign (1617), while Morton wrote years later (1630).

Why did these Native people treat the French sailors so badly? Is this what actually happened, or are Smith and Morton trying to create a certain image? Given the custom of hospitality, had the French done something to elicit this treatment from Native people?

There are numerous accounts of various European ships landing in someone's homeland and sailors disrespecting their Indigenous hosts, sometimes resulting in skirmishes as Native people became disgusted with their behavior. Not to mention the kidnappings and enslaving of Indigenous people that was still going on in the early 1600s.

Is it any wonder Indigenous people grew tired of the attitudes and actions of the Europeans?

Interestingly, neither Smith nor Morton mention any of this. The reactions of Indigenous people are attributed to their so-called "wickedness" and their "mocking," not to normal human responses to the ignorant affronts and intrusive behavior of the French or English.

The "wickedness" mentioned in Morton's quote essentially translates to Indigenous people not being Christian, making it acceptable for them to have been "mightily swept . . . away." Here, Indigenous people are being blamed for their own devastation in the Great Dying.

We may never be able to establish whether the plague of 1616–1618 was intentional or not. However, there is a big difference if we read Smith's passage and accept it verbatim, or if we do some critical analysis and take a deeper look.

It is documented history that much more was involved in the Pilgrims settling here than simply finding a place to practice religious freedom. The *Mayflower* voyage was a financial endeavor paid for by a group called the Merchant Adventurers. Their goals were to establish a colony, obtain the riches (profit) of the land—furs, timber, and gold, were it to be found—and have the colony thrive so that the riches would keep flowing back to Europe. To get control of the land for these purposes, they had to dominate or annihilate Indigenous people. The whole story of the Pilgrims seeking religious freedom became mythologized when it began to be presented as the *only* reason they came here, thereby erasing the rest of this history.

After the Great Dying, disease continued to be used as a weapon of colonization. In western Massachusetts in the late 1700s, Jeffery Amherst gave smallpox-contaminated blankets to the Norwottuck people, knowing they had no immunity and would catch smallpox and die. This was done intentionally to clear the land for European and American settlers. Introducing disease by smallpox-infested blankets or other means was utilized all the way across the country as European settlement advanced westward. This is one of many examples over the last four centuries where Europeans and Americans placed themselves in a position to decide whether Indigenous people lived or died. Is the Doctrine of Discovery at work here?

WHY DIDN'T INDIGENOUS PEOPLE HAVE THE IMMUNITY TO FIGHT OFF THE EUROPEAN DISEASES?

People sometimes ask how long Wampanoag or other Indigenous people lived. They expect to hear about a short life span due to the primitive, backward, barbarous manner in which we supposedly lived, and are often shocked to hear the average age was eighty years, and it was not uncommon for people to reach one hundred.

This information can be very confusing as people measure it against what they thought they knew, or learned in school. How can that be? they ask. The answer is that Wampanoag people grew their food in clean earth—the soil was clean, the air was clean, the waters were clean, the forests, fields, mountains, beaches, everything was clean. This means as nature intended, as nature was created. Our life—lifestyle, life ways—was based on our relationship with the earth, and so was clean.

This clean lifestyle and earth didn't happen randomly, but rather was purposefully constructed. Indigenous people took care of the land in particular ways for thousands and thousands of years, with insight and understanding, customs and practices being passed down over hundreds of generations. Love and respect are two of the main feelings and attitudes held for the land. The first explorers from Europe in the sixteenth and seventeenth centuries described the country as being like Eden or Paradise. This "Eden" happened because of our relationship with the land.

And because we lived in this clean way, keeping and working with everything as created, we did not create or cause infectious diseases. Because we did not have the diseases in the first place, our bodies did not build the immunity, or form the antibodies to fight disease, that happens when one is exposed, creating antibodies that form in the body as a defense. It was not needed. This is why Indigenous people were unable to fight off the diseases when Europeans arrived.

IMPACTS OF FOREIGN DISEASES

Foreign diseases were devastating to Indigenous communities, even beyond the massive loss of life. Entire generations of people died, as the diseases killed adults, elders, children, and babies alike. Some families carried certain knowledge or responsibilities within their communities. Perhaps they had certain herbal knowledge, an understanding of plants and medicine, or they were the people who conducted certain ceremonies. If they all died, what happened to that knowledge or performance of those responsibilities? That knowledge was gone. Families carried knowledge over hundreds of generations, and in a two-year span, it was gone.

In the case of the Great Dying, the deaths of so many in a short period of time also resulted in a huge impact on the land. The relationship between the land and the people was disrupted, then halted altogether. Ancient practices such as farming, foraging, and landscape management, including burning the underbrush and burning over the gardens, came to a stop, at least in the plague-stricken areas. Animal populations were affected because hunting and fishing slowed drastically or stopped. The landscape itself changed and did not flourish as it once had. It became out of balance.

The Pilgrims settling in Wampanoag territory just after the Great Dying interfered with the process of recuperation and regeneration of life as it had been before the plague. "Normal" for Wampanoag people never completely happened again, as the English pushed for more and more land and imposed a multitude of colonial restrictions upon us. Thus the progression of dispossession was established.

LAND PATENTS

Did you know that the Pilgrims were not supposed to land on the site they later named Plimoth? Their original destination was the colony of "Virginia," which included Jamestown and extended north to what is now

New York City, at the mouth of the Hudson River. However, they were blown off course and ended up quite a bit north in the area now named Cape Cod.

If they had landed in "Virginia," they were covered legally—according to English law—by a document known as the first Peirce Patent, issued in February of 1620 and adopted before the *Mayflower* left England. Landing on Cape Cod put them out of English "jurisdiction," and by English law they were here illegally. To cover the interim until their legalities could be updated, the Mayflower Compact was drawn up. This was not a legal document, according to English law, but served as a declaration of self-governance and allegiance to the English crown. Today there is a school of thought that presents the Mayflower Compact as the precursor of the Declaration of Independence and the US Constitution. However, in the 1600s the Pilgrims considered themselves English citizens, believed America belonged to England, and had no thought to create a separate country.

In 1621, therefore, the second Peirce Patent was issued, which John Peirce obtained from the Council of New England. It allowed the Pilgrims seven years to establish the colony of Plimoth Plantation and repay their debt to the Merchant Adventurers. Their payment was not in money but in furs and timber, this being a business arrangement.

John Peirce was the leader of the Merchant Adventurers, the financial backers for the *Mayflower* voyage. Their purpose was to set up colonies and trade to make money, to reimburse their original investments and make a profit. The English government had established the Council of New England as the official body to conduct such business.

The King of England, James I, through the Council of New England, issued the Charter of New England in 1620, which basically stated that all of "America," "from sea to sea," belonged to the king, to England. The king was claiming "America" as a colony, from forty-four degrees latitude to thirty-four degrees latitude, and longitudinally roughly to the Great Lakes. Forty-four degrees is in the area of Truro and Halifax, Nova Scotia, and thirty-four degrees is approximately where Fayetteville and Charlotte, North Carolina, are now. Look at a map to see just how large an area this is. It is also the homeland of a great number of Indigenous nations. England had colonies all over the world, where essentially they were claiming the lands of other people.

The patents for "America" claimed the land of all the people Indigenous to "America," including all the resources of the land. England could do this, by its own rules or laws, as long as no other Christian people had made a claim on "America." This clearly follows the terms in the Doctrine of Discovery.

The Pilgrims were very concerned about the legality in terms of English law of their landing in Wampanoag country, but they gave no thought or consideration to Wampanoag law and customs. They did not understand or even consider that Wampanoag people had laws, governmental structure, and an organized, successful society. This alone tells you that the Pilgrims did not see Wampanoag people as equals. Wampanoag were considered to be "backward" and "primitive," and so incapable of creating a functional culture with laws and structure. Equality does not and cannot exist with such beliefs.

THE TRUTH ABOUT THE FIRST THANKSGIVING

This book addresses many assumptions about and attitudes toward Native people that the English and Europeans held upon first arriving. These have persisted over the last four centuries, passing down over many generations for so long that they are considered truth, and are largely still held today. They have become ingrained in the thinking of Americans, and also many other people around the world! Not only are these notions false, they have become mythologized. America has created an entire story around the arrival of the Pilgrims and their meeting and relationship with the "Indians." While there are elements of truth in this story, most of it is *not what happened.*

One of the biggest myths is that of the "First Thanksgiving." Everyone learned this story: after an arduous and treacherous journey across the sea, the Pilgrims finally arrive in America and are happily greeted and welcomed by the "Indians." In the spring, Squanto teaches them how to plant corn, and when they have their first successful corn harvest that fall, they celebrate with the "First Thanksgiving," inviting the "Indians" to join them in their harvest celebration. Usually, the "Indians" drop out of sight after dinner, and the Pilgrims go on to build America. The "Indians" don't appear again until America begins to head west.

Time for some critical analysis!

First, this myth communicates that the Pilgrims arrived in a "vast," "empty" land. They saw America as a huge wilderness with no civilization, in spite of their awareness of Indigenous people—which makes its own statement. The fact is, the Pilgrims landed and settled in Wampanoag territory, where clearly everyone had not perished in the Great Dying. Indigenous people had complex cultures, with spiritual, social, legal, and political organization in their societies and regarding their lands.

A second part of the myth is that the "Indians" ran down to meet and greet the *Mayflower*'s arrival. This simply did not happen. It was December, and Wampanoag people lived inland in the forests, away from the ocean, during the winter. However, the Pilgrims were observed throughout the winter. They came into someone else's country, started building homes, and setting up a town. Of course Wampanoag people were aware of this going on in their homeland! Otherwise, how would Samoset have known to go into Plimoth in March of 1621? He went in to determine what the Pilgrims were about.

A third part of the myth is that Squanto and all the "Indians" immediately became great friends with the Pilgrims. While it is true that Squanto showed the Pilgrims how to plant corn using herring for fertilizer, this did not happen because the English and the Wampanoag were friends. These were people from two different races, cultures, and countries meeting for the first time, in a colonial-settlement situation. It is a gross oversimplification to say they were friends. "Friends" ignores the events that occurred prior to settlement (see Chapter 4), while pretending that Wampanoag people happily welcomed them— construing acceptance of colonization!

A fourth part of the myth is that the Pilgrims invited the "Indians" to join them in this "First Thanksgiving." Actually, there is only one paragraph that exists in the historical record that describes what has come to be known as the "First Thanksgiving." In a small volume called *Mourt's Relation,* written in 1622, a single passage says that "Massasoit, with some ninety men" came "amongst us." When people elaborate on sources like this, for example, with the Pilgrims inviting the Indigenous people, then history is being made up. This actually distorts history. Analyzing the written word for meaning is one thing. It is another thing entirely to make assumptions about the words that are there.

Fifth, the name "First Thanksgiving" implies that there was a second, and people sometimes mistakenly believe that "Thanksgiving" happened every year to the present day. The harvest event of 1621 happened only once. In 1844, a man named Alexander Young wrote *The Chronicles of the Pilgrim Fathers,* updating the writings of Edward Winslow, author of *Mourt's Relation.* On the page relating the harvest celebration, Young had a footnote at the bottom: "This was the first Thanksgiving." That is where the 1621 event got named as such, more than two hundred years later.

The most dangerous element of myths such as the "First Thanksgiving" is that they hide the history

This painting of the "First Thanksgiving" is the only one known to correctly portray the right numbers of Wampanoag and English people at the 1621 harvest festival.

that actually happened. They oversimplify and omit the "negative," "controversial," "uncomfortable" parts of history, presenting a false image that everything was "peaceful" and "friendly," implying that Indigenous people just accepted all the forces of colonization imposed upon us.

SLAVERY

Indigenous slavery is not nearly as well-recognized as the enslavement of Black people in American history. Indigenous slavery was fully instituted by the

1640s, and many thousands of Indigenous people were forced into it. Like other colonial practices, it was an ongoing system targeting the domination and control of people and, ultimately, the land. As mentioned in Chapter 4, prior to 1620, there were many instances of Indigenous people from coastal tribes in what is now New England being kidnapped and sold into slavery in England or Spain. In southern New England, slavery took the form of forced indenture, where tribal people were put into domestic work (house servant), farming, skilled labor (for instance, a blacksmith), or maritime (whaling) service. Men, women, and children were bonded out—bought and paid for—to perform such services, a practice that continued into the 1800s. There is more information in the "Indenture" section later in this chapter, and also in the "King Philip's War" section in Chapter 8.

DEBT

The creation of debt within Indigenous communities was another imposed colonial system. In our traditional societies, we did not have or need money. Traditional economies depended on the land, the way that we lived and acted in relationship with the land.

This means we provided for ourselves from the land: food, shelter, clothing, and medicine, or other needs. As colonial systems were forced upon us, we lost more and more land, which reduced our ability to provide for our needs ourselves. Being launched into a money economy created dependence on others outside the families or communities.

Because we did not have money or the means to acquire it (in comparison to white society), the English allowed for borrowing. Indigenous people were thrust into this system in order to feed and care for their families. Constant borrowing, however, led to the accumulation of debt, which the English also allowed, that being the plan.

When a family's debt had become too steep, they had two ways of resolving it. One method was to go to their sachem for assistance. Individuals in tribal communities had rights to resources that were held in common by their community—such as land. The sachem could pay the family's debt with a certain amount of land.

And once again, these were not isolated incidences of people getting into debt, but a wholesale process. The sachems got caught in the middle of these situations. As in precontact times, only they had the authority to transfer lands. However, debt payment by the sachems was happening so fast and so frequently that sometimes people didn't even know the land under their feet had been sold for debt.

The sachems requested that people stop accumulating debt, but often circumstances left them no choice if they were going to be able to provide food and other necessities for their families. While people still hunted, fished, farmed, and foraged to sustain themselves, traditional land use practices had been completely interrupted, prevented by fences, laws, and force, and the loss of the land itself.

INDENTURE

Debt could also be paid off through indenture. Generally, indenture is a system in which people go into service with a blacksmith, a carpenter, or someone in a similar profession, in order to learn that trade. Children could enter such a service at about age eight, and remain until age eighteen or twenty-one. They would then be released from indenture, and go on to set up their own business with which to support themselves. This was done in Europe, and was a practice brought to America.

Indenture for Indigenous people was a very different experience. And it became another way to pay

Dorcas Honorable was a Nantucket Wampanoag woman of the 1700s into the 1800s, who was indentured to a white sea captain. She bears the brand of being enslaved on her right cheek.

off debt. Families went to the English court to put one of their children, usually the oldest, into indenture. People did not want to do this, but it left the parents in the home as they were the main support of the family. If one or both parents became indentured, then that was the fate of all the children as well.

Aside from the circumstance of debt, if the English perceived that an Indigenous family could not care for their children, they would remove them to an English household. The English felt they were able—as people who were "civilized" and not "primitive" or "heathens"—to raise children better than their own families. This meant the children would be put into indenture, working as house servants for an English family: cooking, cleaning, caring for children, or tending fields or farm animals. Indigenous people were not usually released by a certain age but kept in indenture for undetermined lengths of time.

Indenture became a form of slavery, with both adults and children caught in this system.

Think about it this way. Your parents may have a mortgage—a type of loan—on your home, which pays for its purchase. People pay mortgages each month, and there are fees for late or missed payments. What if, instead of the late fee, the bank could take you or your brother or sister if missed payments could not be made? How would that affect your family? How would you feel?

REMOVING CHILDREN FROM THEIR HOMES

Prior to the disruptions of colonization, it should be noted, Indigenous people had no issues raising healthy children, families, and communities.

It was only when Indigenous people could not be on the land as they always had to sustain traditional ways of life that the systems of debt and poverty took hold. This is a completely different issue from Moms', Dads', and Grandparents' ability to love and care for their children and families. The English equated this imposed lack of ability to Indigenous parents being lazy, incompetent, or stupid.

So Indigenous children were taken from their families—from all tribes within Massachusetts, Rhode Island, Connecticut—and placed in English homes. These children were separated from everything and everyone they had ever known, and were lonely, homesick, sad, and scared. Separation from family had disastrous consequences. Since they might not get to see their family or community for years, children grew up losing contact and becoming unfamiliar with their own people and cultural ways. The children, especially in earlier times, did not speak English but only their own languages, and were punished and shamed for speaking them. As adults they would not teach the younger ones, to spare them the shaming. Languages that carried worldview and philosophy fell into disuse. People forgot or never learned cultural ways and ceremonies. They were not there for family get-togethers; they never got to go clamming or blue fishing. They didn't learn how to grow corn, or how to find medicines out in the woods. They didn't learn, or forgot, their own songs and dances. They didn't learn how to cook their own foods, or how to use fire. And meanwhile, the English constantly denigrated Indigenous cultures, making the children feel ashamed for being born who they were.

Children grew up alienated from their own people

and cultures, but also were not white people, and were not accepted into white society. Again, this was not done randomly, in isolated cases, but was pervasive throughout the region. This practice disrupted families, communities, and culture.

The practice of removing children from the tribes of first contact on the east coast was likely the beginning of the concept of the boarding schools that were built across this country and in Canada. All of the same elements were utilized, removing children from their homes and transporting them hundreds of miles away. Children were subjected to physical, mental, emotional, and spiritual abuse. The effects of these experiences damaged not only the children who went through them, but tumbled down generations, affecting their children and grandchildren.

LET'S THINK ABOUT THIS:

1. How is it that the King of England thought that he could claim North America? Once again, refer back to the Doctrine of Discovery!

2. In the "Spring" section of "When Life Was Our Own," find two examples of people receiving help they needed from the community.

3. Compare the practice of removing children from their homes with the definition of racism at the beginning of the book.

4. Can you find one example in each season in "When Life Was Our Own" that elaborates on how children were traditionally raised? How do these examples compare to the English assumptions about such Wampanoag traditions?

CHAPTER 7

WHEN LIFE WAS OUR OWN: AUTUMN–TIME OF THE HARVEST

HARVEST TIME IS HERE

Summer was winding down, and the days already shorter. The light had changed, and the air felt different, quiet proclamations of autumn coming in. The heat of the day seems softer in early fall, and the clouds bigger, puffier, white and gray. They still spoke of rain, but soon they would tell of snow, becoming darker and heavier. The trees were still green, and the gardens were full of fresh vegetables. The women spent most days picking the ripe corn, beans, squashes, pumpkins, melons, and sunflowers.

The best ears of corn were set aside for next year's seed. Of the rest, the husks were removed except for three, by which a couple dozen ears were braided into a bundle, making a husk-rope to hang them for drying. Little Bird collected a basketful of the extra husks and showed Strawberry and Punkinseed how to dry and soak them and make corn husk dolls. Before long, the

Freshly harvested ears of corn are braided together so they can be hung to dry for winter meals.

girls had made entire families of corn husk people. They found a place where no one really walked and set them up there, complete with little twig-framed houses and little cleared gardens.

Of course, all the girls spent most of their time helping with the harvest. Mom and Grandma Yellow Sky showed them how to tell which ears would be for seed and which would be dried for food, and to set aside the ones that didn't form completely.

Smiling Dove set the girls up with large bowls, one side of a deer's jawbone, and a whole pile of ears that were partially formed but still had good kernels. She showed them how to use the jawbone to scrape the kernels from the cobs into the bowl, warning them to take their time. The deer's teeth are very sharp and can cut tender skin if you don't watch what you're doing. Little Bird remembered when she was first learning, she was moving too fast, confident she had things under control. Before even realizing it, she had a big gash on her thumb! Yellow Sky cleaned the cut, put on some medicine, and covered the wound. Her thumb was pretty sore for a few days, and she wasn't able to work. Now Little Bird watched the little girls very closely, not wanting them to have a similar experience! When their bowls were full, they spread the kernels out on bulrush mats to dry in the sun. It felt like they had been scraping for half the day, but the pile of corn didn't look any smaller. There was such a good harvest this year!

Strawberry especially liked going through the fields, picking all the dry bean pods. They crinkled in her hand as she picked them, and she was careful not to break them and spill the beans! She happily showed Punkinseed this new accomplishment of picking pods and keeping them whole. This was their first time helping with the harvest. When their baskets were full, they went over to the outdoor kitchen and shucked all the beans into the storage bag that

Smiling Dove put out for them. As the days passed, more and more beans were ready for picking. Strawberry, even though she had grown so much this year (after all, she was six!), could have still fit into that storage bag, and it was close to half full!

River, Red Dawn, and Woodchuck helped the girls bring in the larger pumpkins and squashes. There was already a huge pile under the kitchen arbor. There was so much food harvested! Smiling Dove, Blue Heron, Stands Strong, and Yellow Sky were hard at work slicing the vegetables into thin strips or coils to dry, saving the seeds for next year. Most of the squashes would be dried for meals over the winter. All the kids helped, making the work go quickly. Some people were already making trips back to the winter village to fill the storage pits there. And a lot was left in storage at the summer homes, for when people returned next spring.

Little Bird's entire family helped with the harvest from all their fields. It was a lot of work to braid corn, shuck beans, and slice pumpkins and squashes. A lot of care was taken to make sure all this food dried thoroughly and did not get damp or wet in any way. It had to be completely dry so it would not spoil. Mom and Grandma Yellow Sky worked very carefully to spill not one corn kernel or one bean, demonstrating that care to the girls. Leaving spilled food on the ground just wasn't done—showing respect for the plants that gave them food.

Strong Bear and Tall Pine had gone hunting that morning and returned with two geese. They plucked and cleaned them and got them roasting over the fire. Smiling Dove set a big kettle on, with fresh corn and beans. After a while, she added some pumpkin strips. Strawberry's mouth watered already! Pumpkin was one of her favorite foods (after strawberries, of course). (And blueberries and raspberries.) (Blackberries!) (Cherries . . . grapes . . . beach plums.) (The tart cranberries that make your whole face pucker!) Anyway, pumpkin was one of her favorite foods. The different squashes were always good, but pumpkin was much sweeter!

RUSH SEASON

Smiling Dove and Yellow Sky continued with the corn harvest. They also gathered mint, sumac, and other wild plants, for food or medicine. They collected clams, mussels, and quahogs to dry and smoke, to put away for the winter. Blue Heron and Stands Strong loaded all the girls into a boat and headed up the river. At the spot where it widened out into a pond, both bulrush and cattail grew in abundance. Every year, they cut enough bulrush to make three or four new mats. That's about eighty bundles of reeds, which hardly put a dent in the whole field of bulrush! Blue Heron and the little girls stayed in the boat, entering the bulrush field from the water. With their Auntie's guidance, the girls offered tobacco on the water and whispered thanksgiving to the reeds who were giving their lives so the people could have beautiful mats on the walls of their houses, keeping them warm and toasty throughout the winter. They had to reach into the water to cut the rushes near their roots. Auntie could grab a large number of reeds in a handful, as she deftly cut them and laid them in the bottom of the boat. For Strawberry and Punkinseed, a handful was about four reeds. Together they cut a bundle's worth of reeds, while Blue Heron cut three!

Stands Strong and Little Bird walked into the water at the river's edge. They offered their tobacco and prayers, and then began to cut their way into the reeds. They laid the bulrush in individual piles, to tie and bundle later. The farther they went into the reeds, the looser and "swimmier" the river bottom became under their feet. They weren't walking on the sandy bottom anymore, but the grown-together roots of the bulrush and the other plants. Stands Strong and Little Bird felt their way along with their feet testing each step to make sure the root-mesh would hold them. All of a sudden, everyone heard a shriek. All eyes turned to Little Bird, who suddenly had become much shorter than when she had entered the reeds. . . . She had misjudged her step and her feet broke through the root-mesh. She was in the water up to her waist! Her feet were not touching the bottom but kicking freely in the cold fresh river current. Her Auntie backtracked and helped Little Bird lift herself up and regain her footing. She advised her to place her feet near the roots of all the plants, where the mesh would support her weight. Well! She would remember that lesson! She didn't relish the thought of a big snapping turtle happening along to chomp on her toes!

The rest of the morning remained uneventful. The day was hot, but a good cloud cover kept the sun from beating down on them in the open water. And there was a refreshing breeze everyone was grateful for. When they had cut forty bundles, they decided to return home to begin processing these reeds and collect more another day. They loaded all the bundles into the boat, and Blue Heron maneuvered the vessel back down the river toward the planting fields. Stands

Strong walked with the girls on the path that ran beside the river, the boat always in sight.

Little Bird reflected on the day. In spite of falling into the river, she had seen three frogs, who bounded away from her into a thicket; one water snake who also preferred to head in another direction; and a lot of different spiders, including one that was as big as her hand. That eight-legged relative scuttled away from her as well . . . for which she silently offered a little prayer of thanks! She would have to ask Grandpa Singing Wolf to tell her about that kind of spider.

While the women and girls were gathering bulrush, the men and boys built drying racks for them. The women arrived home late in the day and left all the bulrush right in the boat for the night. Tall Pine, Strong Bear, and Walks in the Moonlight had gotten two turkeys, and had them roasting, along with a pot of corn soup. Everyone got together for dinner, and Yellow Sky offered the prayer before eating. Between three hungry families, there wasn't much left on the turkeys, but the bones would make a nice broth for tomorrow's stew!

Little Bird helped Strawberry and Punkinseed get into bed, before sinking down into the soft furs herself. They were sleeping in the house now, with just a small fire, as the nights were getting cooler. A balmy breeze found its way inside, brushing Little Bird's cheek, lulling her to sleep. The three boys walked back to Stands Strong's house, ready for bed after a long day cutting saplings and building racks, followed by a hearty meal. The parents, aunts and uncles, and grandparents stayed up awhile, talking quietly around the fire. The night sounds added to their comfort: the crackling of the fire, chirping of the crickets, the deeper chirp of little tree frogs, the occasional croaks of bullfrogs, and the breeze rustling through the pines. Everyone turned in very shortly. Tomorrow would be another long day, preparing the bulrush.

By the time Little Bird, Strawberry, and Punkin-seed awoke the next morning, Smiling Dove, Blue Heron, Stands Strong, and Yellow Sky already had the huge clay kettles set over fires and were heating water to boil the bulrush. Boiling removed the sap from them, so they absorbed any humidity or mois-ture in the air. This is how the mats made the homes cooler in hot weather and warmer in cold. The girls had some breakfast and got ready to help with the bulrush. Once boiled, the reeds were spread out to cool, then tied into small bundles and laid on the drying racks. It was a very hot end-of-summer day, but the boiling kettles had been set in the shade by the river. Fory large bundles was a lot of boiling and rebundling! Strawberry and Punkinseed held a math discussion. Half of a large bundle would fit into a kettle, multiplied by four kettles, so two bundles could be boiled at a time. They looked at each other, wide-eyed, then looked at all the reeds, and looked back at each other. They got a little lost in the middle of the math equation but figured this was a three- or four- or even a five-day project! Maybe six? A whole lot of boiling going on in Green Pine town!

This was Strawberry's and Punkinseed's first time helping with the bulrush. Little Bird, on the other hand, had already been doing this every summer for a few years now. She helped her Mom, Grandma, and Aunties put bunches of reeds into the kettles. It took constant attention to feed the fires and maintain a red-hot bed of coals to keep the water boiling. More water had to be added every so often, as it boiled down. Pouring in cooler water required great care so it didn't hit the sides of a hot kettle, causing it to crack and break. Not the desired outcome for a great pot of scalding water!

The weather was with them, and they finished boiling and bundling the bulrush in five days' time. The first bundles laid on the rack were actually almost dry. If it remained sunny, they would be completely dry in a couple of days. Some of the women might start weaving mats right away, having time before everyone left at the end of harvest for the winter village. The rest of the reeds were put in the storage building, where people also stored their usable cattail mats.

CATTAIL TIME

Once the bulrush harvest was completed, and all boiled and stored, it was time to collect cattails. The people had been using these mats for thousands of years to cover their homes—because they worked. Cattail mats are ideally suited to protect homes from wind, rain, and stormy weather. And the more they are harvested, the more they will grow.

The women rose early, got the fire going, and made breakfast before waking the girls. Everyone ate together and got ready to go and cut cattails. They would need 120 to 150 bundles to make a complete "set" of new mats, which was done every year for the summer home. The mats were of different lengths, depending on what part of the house they covered. They were as tall as the height of the reeds they were made from—some even taller than Tall Pine!

Yellow Sky, Smiling Dove, Blue Heron, and Stands

Strong thought they should cut as many bundles as they could on this first trip. This swamp was just up the river from where they had cut bulrush, and they again took a boat, a longer one to hold the size of the cattail bundles. Little Bird would help Strawberry and Punkinseed on their first venture into the cattail swamp. When they got there, they offered their prayers and left tobacco on the water. Grandma Yellow Sky and Blue Heron worked from the boat, while Smiling Dove, Stands Strong, Little Bird, and the two younger girls walked in from the land. This was an easy swamp compared to the bulrush. You could walk right in and not even get your feet wet.

The women cut their way into the swamp, making piles of cattails as they went along. Little Bird showed Strawberry and Punkinseed how to tie the piles into neat bundles. The cattail bundles were much larger than the bulrush, so the little girls coordinated a double-team effort, as they weren't quite big enough to straddle and tie a bundle alone. They followed the women, who suddenly veered off and left a grouping of reeds standing in place. As the little girls quizzically considered this, Little Bird directed them to look up at the tips of the cattails. Swaying in the breeze on webs built between the leaves were four giant black-and-yellow spiders with silver furry backs

The girls watched frozen in place as one of them had just caught a grasshopper, and was wrapping the struggling insect in his—her?—webbing. Strawberry looked at the spiders and looked at her hand. A shiver went down her back as she realized how huge they were! Punkinseed sprinted over to her mother's side. Little Bird chuckled at the girls' first introduction to these creatures. She knew the spiders would not bother them, and they would be careful not to pile cattails near the standing ones. There was no need to be a spider home-wrecker.

So Punkinseed and Strawberry spent the day following Little Bird's example, and bent and piled, and then bent and tied. Bend and pile, bend and tie. Bend and pile, bend and tie. Earlier that morning, that task did not sound like such a difficult thing. But after doing it for quite a long time, the little girls gained a new respect for this work. The sun was starting to lower, so they decided to pile all the bundles in the boat, and Yellow Sky and Blue Heron would paddle back down the river toward home. They had gotten sixty bundles in one trip—almost half as many as they would need. Smiling Dove, Stands Strong, and Little Bird took the tired little ones by the hands, and began the walk home.

Grandma and Blue Heron were just pulling in

when the rest arrived at the fields. Strong Bear, Walks in the Moonlight, Tall Pine, and the boys had come in earlier from fishing, and were roasting a huge blue-fish over the fire. Smiling Dove and Blue Heron put a kettle on to start some dried beans. Later, they would add fresh corn, squash, and green beans. Yellow Sky thought the stew would be delicious with a nice wal-nut gravy, and ground some into flour in the mortar. Little Bird helped Grandma, stirring in the flour to flavor and thicken the stew. The little girls, however, faced a dilemma: they were too hungry to fall asleep, yet fighting to keep their eyes open!

When the fish was done, Little Bird helped her Dad slide it off the spit and into a large serving bowl. The women served everyone fish and stew, a wel-come hot meal on a cool end-of-summer evening. Strawberry, Punkinseed, and Woodchuck did man-age to get some dinner down before succumbing to the weight of their eyelids. Grandma Yellow Sky and all the Moms cleaned up after dinner, while the Dads put the kids to bed. The next day would begin the work of splitting, bundling, and drying the cattails.

Cattails have several leaves growing in stalks from their roots. There are about eight leaves on a stalk, which need to be separated or split to individual leaves. They are then placed into piles of shorter or longer leaves. Little Bird showed the little kids (all the sleepyheads) how to carefully split the leaves from the stalks without breaking them. Broken reeds cannot be used for mat making, as their full length is needed. When still green, the leaves are stiff and brittle, and care is needed when separating them.

Little Bird demonstrated her splitting technique to the younger kids, sliding her thumb easily and gently under the outermost leaf, peeling it from the stalk. The little kids each took a cattail plant, carefully swinging the long reeds around so that they were holding the root end in one hand. They had to work apart from each other, to avoid standing on or damaging each other's reeds. As the children began splitting, Little Bird warned them to watch out—the edges of the cattail leaves are sharp enough to give you a good scratch!

Everyone settled to work on the enormous piles of cattails, finding their rhythm of splitting and piling, splitting and piling. It wasn't long before the little kids realized how much work was really involved. It didn't take long at all to split a single cattail, but it took the four of them half the morning to do one pile. It seemed like the great pile of sixty bundles would take—now, let's see, Strawberry calculated—about a thousand years!

While the families split cattails, Strong Bear, Tall Pine, and Walks in the Moonlight went out fishing and shellfishing again. They left very early in the morning before everyone else was awake. The times for lots of fresh fish became fewer as autumn moved in. Soon hunting season would begin. So the "splitting team" was Grandma Yellow Sky and Grandpa Singing Wolf, Smiling Dove, Blue Heron, and Stands Strong; Red Dawn, River, and Woodchuck; and Little Bird, Strawberry, and Punkinseed. The little kids all tackled one pile together, picking up a little speed as they got the feel of the work into their fingers. Once all the reeds in a bundle were split, the piles of short and long ones were tied into smaller bundles and laid on the drying racks. It would take several days before the cattails were dry and no longer green, but the color of dry corn husks. Then they would be stored until mat weaving time.

Even with everyone helping, it still took a few days to split the sixty bundles and get them on the drying racks. They were all turned every day so they would dry evenly. Like the bulrush, they were brought inside the storehouse if it was going to rain. Getting wet would make them moldy and useless for mats. There were always dead, broken leaves on the stalks, or those that got broken during splitting. These were spread out over the cornfields, to be burned later on.

HARVEST CEREMONIES

The remaining days at the summer homes were spent in the gardens harvesting in the early mornings before the sun got too hot. It was a busy time, ensuring all food was collected and preserved. Strawberry hoped they might find one more juicy sweet melon hidden under the leaves in the garden, but they were long gone now. The rest of the cattails were cut, split, and dried over the next half cycle of the moon. The women went through the woods gathering medicine plants, food plants including acorns and different nuts, many kinds of roots and tubers, and the last of the beach plums and grapes. They went down to the bogs and checked on the cranberries. They would soon be red, ripe, and ready for the picking.

The clan mothers came together to plan the Harvest Ceremonies. They were done to thank the Earth for everything she had given the people: all the fish and shellfish; all the corn and vegetables; the berries, nuts and roots; the medicine plants; the plants used to make so many different tools or cordage; the deer, ducks, geese, turkeys, bears. And the melons! The ceremonies were to thank all of these beings, each and every one, for giving their lives so people could live them's. The enormity of this giving was imbued in the smallest children and babies, so they grew up with the proper respect and understanding to keep the world in balance.

After all the ceremonies, feasting, and dancing, everyone headed home. It was a lovely sight to see the glowing fires showing through the open doors, smoke wafting from the tops of the houses, floating away on gentle breezes. The moon was starting to rise, a huge orange ball climbing into the night sky. Grandmother Moon slowly rose into a field of a million stars. Strawberry and Punkinseed had been discussing that, and thought that seemed like the right number, even though between the two of them, they were running out of fingers! Strong Bear stoked the fire, and everyone gathered around. The little girls snuggled in Grandma's and Grandpa's laps, sharing their fur capes. No one spoke a word, just watched the moon rise, immersed in the sounds of the night. There were still crickets and other insects, their chirping and humming seeming much more hushed now. Somebody in the river nearby splashed and plopped back in the water, while all heads turned as a twig snapped not too far into the forest. Was perhaps a black bear out for a last evening before his winter

Grandmother Moon got higher and high[er,] color changed from bright orange to the softe[r] of salmon, eventually becoming a pale yellow[.] Grandma Yellow Sky and Grandpa Singin[g] wrapped the girls in their own furs, and they [went] out to the beach to see the harvest moon in [the] sky. Everyone was silent as they sat on the [sand] basking in the bright, moonlit night. The qu[iet] full moon night always gave Little Bird goose [bumps.] Such times were one of her favorite things! G[randma] and Grandpa pointed out how the stars had c[hanged] their place in the sky again. The girls named [the] stars and the patterns that they formed, review[ing]

Firelight, moonlight, reflections on the water after a long and wonderful day!

ancient history of the people. After a long time, they got up to return home. Everyone was ready for sleep, even though it was hard to bid the beautiful moon good night.

BECOMING AUTUMN

The leaves of all the trees were changing color, showing bright red, orange, yellow, and gold. The air was crisp and fresh, the nights cooler, and the sun setting earlier. Everyone slept in the houses now, keeping the fire going all night long. All the kids loved the feeling of snuggling down, feeling the cool air slip away as the furs wrapped them in warmth, listening to the fire crackle and snap, lulling them to sleep. No doubt, now that summer was over, autumn was here, and winter was on its way!

Everyone from all the planting sites had been making regular trips back to the winter village, bringing their baskets of dried food to store. The men checked the longhouses, making sure the bark coverings and frames were in good repair. The women checked the inside bulrush mats, replacing any worn ones with those made this fall. The old mats would line the storage pits, keeping dampness from the food, or be used on the floors in the houses. Nothing went to waste.

Yellow Sky took all the girls out to check on the milkweed and dogbane plants. These were two of the plants used to make string and rope for mat making or netting, fish line, or anything that needed tying (like cattail bundles: bend and pile, bend and tie!). Some of their stalks were completely dried out, but many were not. They would return another day. They decided to walk down along the beach, one last visit before leaving for the winter village. Huge waves crashed upon the shore, the water rushing high up on the beach. The air was heavy with salt spray, and they turned their faces into the wind to breathe in the freshness.

Everyone at the planting sites was taking down the cattail and bulrush mats from their houses. If the cattail mats were still usable, they were rolled up and put in the storage house. Ones that were not usable would be burned and worked into the garden soil. Little Bird helped Yellow Sky take their cattail mats down, while Strawberry and Punkinseed rolled them up and tied them. The mats are very light, and the little girls each took an end to carry them to the storage house. They soon discovered that they could carry two mats at a time that way. After a number of trips, the girls were quite proud of their two-girl cattail mat transportation system!

So it wasn't long before the little girls, Little Bird,

and Grandma had all the cattail mats down and safely stored. Next, they took down the bulrush mats on the inside of the house. Smiling Dove, Stands Strong, and Blue Heron had all been helping each other pack up all their bed furs, cooking utensils, tools, hides, clothing, anything that was going back to the winter village. Everybody helped carry everything, but it would still take a few trips. The men and boys went to get the last of the families' things. On this final trip, they would sink all the boats down into the mud of the rivers or ponds. The sediment would keep them from rotting or freezing and cracking.

Grandpa Singing Wolf stayed at the winter home with his daughters and grandchildren. He seemed to have no energy and was not his usual self, offering to help anybody with whatever they might be doing.

Each family had their own space in the winter longhouse, and Smiling Dove, Blue Heron, and Stands Strong each started the fires in their areas. The three families were next to each other, and with other relatives coming in, it was already starting to warm up inside. The next job was to put the bulrush mats back up on the walls. Then the house would really heat up! All the Moms, with Little Bird, Punkinseed, and Strawberry helping, accomplished this task in a short time. Smiling Dove, Blue Heron, and Stands Strong

Taking the last of the cattail mats from the summer home.

returned to their own areas to put things away and start dinner. There was plenty of leftover roast fish, goose meat, corn, beans, and squash to make hot soup on a chilly autumn day.

FROM GIRL TO WOMAN

Smiling Dove and Grandma Yellow Sky had watched Little Bird all spring and summer. She was only twelve, but they noticed how she went about daily activities with a calm confidence. She was becoming an accomplished cook, and often made meals for her entire family. She had already learned how to skin deer and other animals, and to tan hides to make clothing and fur blankets. Grandma Yellow Sky was very pleased with her knowledge thus far of plants and preparing medicines; also preparing plants like cattail, bulrush, dogbane, and milkweed for weaving. And she could weave! Some of Little Bird's favorite things to do were weaving baskets, mats, bags, and sashes. She loved working with the clay and making pottery. And decorating clothing with paint designs or porcupine quill work. She was very aware and made sure her pouch always had tobacco or cornmeal or sage or sweetgrass. Little Bird loved the ocean and going shellfishing or fishing. She worried when helping her Mom that every last clam or quahog or mussel made it into a stew or got over the fire to smoke. She loved going to all the ceremonies and was beginning to be asked to help. She had carried water for the Harvest Ceremonies.

So her Mom and Grandma, and her Aunties Blue Heron and Stands Strong, watched her grow. Girls only a few years older than Little Bird got married and started their own families. Little Bird was learning and changing, becoming her own person, becoming a woman living in her community.

GRANDPA AND THE MEDICINE MAN

Smiling Dove noticed that Grandpa Singing Wolf had been lying down the whole time everyone had been tying mats up and getting their spaces squared away. Grandma Yellow Sky sat with him, trying to get him to drink some sage tea. Grandpa wouldn't take it, and hardly seemed awake. He was also coughing and having some trouble breathing, which caused everyone great concern.

Since Grandpa wouldn't take the tea, Smiling Dove went out and walked over to the home of Eagle Heart, the medicine man, or healer, of their village. He invited her in, and she offered him a pouch of tobacco, a good-size basket of dried corn, and a freshly caught and cleaned turkey. She explained to him how sick her Dad had become, and Eagle Heart made preparations to come and treat him. He gathered up certain dried herbs he had stored and walked back over to Smiling Dove's house with her.

Eagle Heart set up his "treatment area" where Grandpa was lying down. He laid the herbs out on a deerskin and asked Smiling Dove to heat up two different pots of water. Little Bird went with her to get the water, as everyone else gathered around sitting on the opposite bed. Grandma Yellow Sky was hardly keeping back her tears, she was so upset about Grandpa. They had been together their entire lives, since they were teenagers, and were now both around eighty. The little girls were getting upset at seeing their Grandma crying. They had never seen her this way before. Grandpa Rabbit's wife, Strong Bear and Tall Pine's mother, had died a number of years ago, but Strawberry and Punkinseed were babies at that time and did not remember.

When the water in each of the pots had begun to boil, Eagle Heart put some herbs into one of the kettles. In the other, he put two great handfuls of another herb. After they had simmered for a while, he removed them from the water, and made a poultice for Grandpa's chest. Eagle Heart covered Grandpa with a fur blanket to hold the heat in as long as possible. Then he poured Grandpa another cup of tea. Grandma helped him spoon that into Singing Wolf's mouth, and eventually he got it all down. Grandpa fell sound asleep. After a while, Eagle Heart removed the poultice, and rubbed a different medicine on Grandpa's chest and throat. Strawberry stood at Eagle Heart's knee, watching every move, fascinated with the work he was doing. She had no idea what he rubbed on Grandpa's chest. It didn't really have a smell, was a light color, and was thick and oily. The medicine man pulled the fur back up over Grandpa's chest.

Once Grandpa was asleep, Smiling Dove offered Eagle Heart some dinner. He said a prayer of thanks for the meal and ate heartily, so much so that Smiling Dove had to make another pot of stew. Strong Bear and the other men and boys had not yet returned with the rest of the things from the summer home, and they would be hungry.

It wasn't long before everyone heard Strong Bear, Tall Pine, and Walks in the Moonlight coming in with Red Dawn, River, and Woodchuck. They had already heard about Grandpa's illness by the time they got to the house. When they saw Grandpa asleep with Eagle Heart sitting next to him, they quieted down and asked what had happened. Smiling Dove told them how Grandpa had been coughing and couldn't breathe, and she had gone and asked the medicine man to come and tend to him. Eagle Heart at that point held a tobacco ceremony with everyone, praying for Singing Wolf's return to health, and for the meal the men were about to have. Reassured that Grandpa was doing better, the men and boys each got a bowl of stew, and sat down to eat and talk with Eagle Heart.

Finally, after a long day of carrying everything back to the winter home, the children all went into their own families' places, and were soon sound asleep. The adults sat up with Eagle Heart to keep an eye on Grandpa. He sat next to Grandpa, staying with him through the entire night, in case another poultice was needed.

Grandma was very tired and lay down next to her husband to try and get some rest. Only one time during the night did Eagle Heart have to make another poultice for Grandpa's chest, after which he again rubbed on the thick oily medicine. As the night went on, Grandpa ceased coughing, and his breathing became easy.

By morning, Grandpa was awake and feeling so-o-o much better. He was even able to eat some breakfast. Eagle Heart left after that, leaving Grandma and Smiling Dove with some of the poultice herbs and oily rub in case they should need them again. While exhausted from staying up all night, everyone was very relieved that Grandpa was on the mend! Yellow Sky and Strong Bear and Smiling Dove slept in that morning with Grandpa, not waking until well after midday. Little Bird and Strawberry went to their Auntie Blue Heron's space when they got up and had some breakfast with River and Punkinseed. Both girls tended the fire at their home, to make sure everybody stayed warm. Grandpa was better, and they had to keep him that way!

LAST WALK FROM THE SUMMER HOME

Because everyone had been so worried about Grandpa Singing Wolf's illness, Strong Bear and the rest had not had a chance to tell their families about their return trip from the planting fields. They had seen an unusual number of animals, or indications of their presence, on their walk home. They had seen a lot of deer or heard them going through the woods. They had followed their tracks and seen where they had nibbled on the branches of trees. They saw some very fresh tracks of a black bear. At one point, Walks in the Moonlight stopped the others, as they heard the bear in the distance breaking branches as he walked. They could hear him huffing, too. . . . Maybe he was closer than they originally thought! They listened quietly for a bit, but the bear did not seem to be traveling in their direction.

Red Dawn pointed out other tracks to the younger boys. River and Woodchuck followed rabbit, squirrel, raccoon, and skunk tracks. They followed their little trails into the trees, hoping to find a warren, nest, den, or burrow. Like the deer, these animals were eaten for their meat, and their fur used to make pouches, coats, or blankets. It took a skilled hand to remove the skunk's scent glands so that the meat wouldn't be tainted and the fur would remain odorless!

All of a sudden, Woodchuck called out to everyone else. Were these elk tracks he was seeing? Uncle Tall Pine confirmed that yes, they were looking at elk tracks. They were much larger than deer tracks and left a deeper impression in the ground. Tall Pine asked Red Dawn about the tracks. Red Dawn studied them for a moment, then followed them a little ways up the path. He told them the elk was a male and took an approximate guess as to how much he weighed. The elk seemed to be just walking along, unconcerned, no worries. Red Dawn followed the tracks farther and saw where they left the path and turned into the woods. At that point, the tracks became farther apart and turned up the dirt, like the elk had started to run. Red Dawn returned to his family. Perhaps the elk had heard the bear, too! But tracking him would wait for another day, as they had to get home with the families' things. But this was still pretty exciting, as elk weren't usually this far south.

They did venture down from up north from time to time, but it was not a usual thing. Red Dawn decided he would certainly come back to see where the elk was going, and he dropped a pinch of tobacco on his path.

CHAPTER 8

COLONIZATION, CONTINUED: ABUNDANCE OR DESTRUCTION?

LAND: INDIGENOUS RELATIONSHIP

Chapter 4 discussed the different explorers who came into the region in the 1500s and early 1600s. Many of these sailors wrote very detailed descriptions of all the places that they visited. This is one way we know what the landscape looked like then, since it is very different now.

The sailors describe the vastness of the forests and name many different kinds of trees. They could be six feet or more in diameter and a hundred feet or taller in height. This was an average size for trees in old growth forests. The sailors describe the waters, the bays and rivers, and the many, many freshwater springs, which is where people got their drinking water. They describe the incredible variety of animals, birds, and fish. A single flock of pigeons could number a million. One writer noted that when the herring came up the rivers in the spring to spawn, they were so numerous that you could walk across the river on their backs.

There were cedar trees and swamps, white pine, red pine, larch, spruce, oak, ash, beech, birch, cherry, maple, walnut, hickory, elm, chestnut, butternut, and sassafras, to name some. There were grapevines, sumac, viburnum, witch hazel, raspberries, blackberries, beach plums, blueberries, huckleberries, and strawberries. There was mint, wild onion and garlic, milkweed greens, burdock, dock, and lamb's-quarters. There were huge ocean fish such as cod, bluefish, haddock, halibut, and bass, and seals and whales. There were flounder and eels. There were pickerel, perch, and trout. There were quahogs, clams, oysters, mussels, and razor clams. There were deer, black bear, wolf, fox, bobcat, squirrel, rabbit, raccoon, and mice. There were cattails, bulrush, milkweed, and dogbane. This is just a very small list of the plants and animals that Indigenous people in this area used for food, clothing, medicines, housing materials, tools, and many other items that made up everyday life.

Here is another math equation to give a sense of what the landscape was like. Remember that prior to the plague of 1616, Wampanoag people had a population of approximately 70,000, who lived in 69 villages, each village having an average of 1,000 people. How large an area of land would 1,000 people need to live on, considering the way of life?

Let's say each family (an average family being 6 people) had one and a half acres for their garden. That's 250 acres for the planting areas, approximately. In the winter villages, people lived in longhouses that could be 100 feet long, holding 8 to 10 families. Let's say 10 families, for the purposes of our math. So there would also be 167 families (1,000 people divided by 6) divided by 10 families in a longhouse, resulting in 17 longhouses.

How many acres to hold 17 of these buildings? Two longhouses could fit on an acre, leaving room around each so they are not right on top of each other. This means one winter village site could be about 9 or 10 acres.

Then there is all the land where people hunted, fished, and gathered strawberries, blueberries, cranberries, cattails, bulrush, and cedar poles. One cedar swamp could be 20 or 30 miles long. There were huge areas of woods, fields, marshes, swamps, natural bogs, coastal beaches and estuaries, salt and freshwater ponds and lakes, rivers, streams, and springs. How much land do all the beings that people depended on—deer, bear, cedar swamps, forests—need to live the way Creator intended? The village areas were not all the same size, but their boundaries could encompass 50 to 75 square miles.

Two of the largest remaining Wampanoag communities today are Mashpee on Cape Cod, Massachusetts, and Aquinnah on Martha's Vineyard. Mashpee is about 27 square miles in size, which is much smaller than the size of the original village. Aquinnah is about 4 square miles, approximately one fifth of the size of the original village. But these numbers will give you an idea of the land areas of the Wampanoag towns. This is what it took to support the 1,000 people, providing for all their needs. In "When Life Was Our Own," what was the size of the strawberry field?

Indigenous people hold the concept that we and the land are one thing. Wampanoag people from the 1600s (and later) (and now) have traditionally believed that we could not be separated from the land. This is reflected in the structure of the Wampanoag language, because this has always been so. When Wampanoag people say they are from a certain place—one of the sixty-nine villages—the word meaning "to be from a place" means that we originate from that place, that our DNA comes from that place, from that earth.

If we take care of the earth in the way that the Creator has instructed us, then we also take care of ourselves. If we respect Creation, then we respect ourselves. If we respect ourselves, then we respect Creation. Creation is everything that the Creator has made, and how everything is interrelated and nothing is separate from anything else.

LAND: LACK OF RELATIONSHIP

This section addresses several aspects of colonization and describes a very different relationship with the land than that of Indigenous people. What are the differences? What are the impacts of these activities on Indigenous people? How do these topics demonstrate lack of relationship with the land?

SETTLEMENT

Creating a settlement, as the Pilgrims did at Patuxet in 1620, means establishing a colony. A colony, as discussed previously, is a place designed to ultimately yield profit. That might be in the form of timber, furs, sassafras, or other resources of the land. This was done with no acknowledgment of the protocol that required negotiation with Indigenous leaders first. It was also done with no understanding of how Indigenous people related to and used the land.

The Pilgrims chose to build their homes in an area where fields had already been cleared for planting. They knew people had lived there and it wasn't "empty land." They were on the grounds of the village of Patuxet, one of many that had been completely wiped out by the plague of 1616. The Pilgrims were likely creating their settlement among the bones of victims of the Great Dying. It is quite interesting that this is not mentioned in any of their writings.

Wampanoag people observed the Pilgrims throughout their first winter, and were aware of how many English there were, how many passed away, and how many survived until spring. Fifty of the 102 who arrived on the *Mayflower* lived through that first winter.

In the spring of 1621, Massasoit of Pokanoket (one of the sixty-nine villages, now Bristol and Warren, Rhode Island), through Samoset and Tisquantum, made contact with the English, eventually entering into an alliance of mutual protection. Massasoit allowed them to stay on Patuxet land and build Plimoth Plantation. They had their first successful harvest that fall, having grown corn obtained from Wampanoag people. They slowly became more solidly established, and by 1623, just three years later, were already wanting more land.

Taking Indigenous people's lands was part of a system that also dictated many aspects of how we lived: the type of houses we should live in, the clothing we should wear, how we wore our hair, how we worshipped, how we should work, how we should work the land. We were told we should do all these things like the English; we should be like the English.

DISEASES AND EPIDEMICS CONTINUE

Throughout the 1600s, a devastating epidemic occurred in every decade throughout the region. While these illnesses affected the English, Indigenous people suffered more losses because we still did not have immunity against them. During the middle and latter part of the century, English people poured into the Boston area by the shipload, while Indigenous populations declined because of the diseases. The new people coming in wanted more and more land— European settlement had gone way beyond the boundaries of Plimoth Plantation. Boston was established in 1630, with some fifty other English towns subsequently fanning out from the Boston and Plymouth areas, including on Cape Cod and the islands of Martha's Vineyard and Nantucket—all Wampanoag territory.

CATTLE, CORN, PIGS, AND CLAMS

With the English came their livestock: cattle, pigs, goats, sheep, chickens. These animals came from Europe and are not indigenous to this country. As in England, they were used for meat, eggs, wool, and hides.

More Europeans coming here also meant more livestock. This created continual problems for Indigenous people. Throughout the 1600s, the English continued to obtain more land, clear-cutting it for farms to raise their animals and grow crops, both those received from Indigenous people and those brought from Europe. The English did not recognize, or even consider, Indigenous people's relationship with the land. English activities on the land were completely disruptive to very ancient Indigenous ways. They also did not consider the long-term effects of the clear-cutting, the disturbance to the soil of tearing out tree stumps, or the damage to the families of plants and animals in those areas, and how this affects the rainfall and flow of water: the systems Creator put in place.

There are many old court documents from the 1600s where Wampanoag and other Indigenous people lodged complaints about the English cows who trod through their gardens, trampling and destroying the cornfields. They created even more damage as they roamed throughout the countryside. English pigs made their way down to the seashore, where at low tides they would snuffle up the clam beds. This happened consistently enough to significantly affect Indigenous food supplies. Wampanoag people were asking for the English to contain their own animals.

What was the response of the English courts?

FENCES

Wampanoag people were told that they should put up fences around their gardens to keep the cows and the pigs out.

Fencing was not an Indigenous concept. Nature (Creation) was maintained as created—without fences. We did not keep animals the way the English did: barred into small (relatively speaking) areas for the convenience of humans.

By contrast, Indigenous people hunted to get meat. This was not because we couldn't think of such a "convenient" way to keep animals. Rather, it was about our understanding of the world and respecting animals as our relatives, about acknowledging their right to live their lives as given them by the Creator. So we did not corral them in unnatural ways. When it was time to hunt to feed our families, we did so with prayer and ceremony to honor and thank the lives being taken— lives being given up so we can live. Because we take those lives, we have responsibility. If we hunt deer, we are responsible for keeping the forest the way that the deer need it, as it was created, to sustain their lives— where they live and have their babies and generations.

The attitude of the courts begs the question: Why did it become the responsibility of Wampanoag people to tend to English livestock? Why didn't the English take responsibility for their own animals? Why didn't they see fit to keep their fences in good repair, or keep their gates closed? Why didn't they apologize or offer reparation for the damage to Wampanoag fields, clam beds, and lands?

This seems thoughtless, rude, and unneighborly at best. Perhaps it wasn't that thoughtless, but done with certain intention.

DEEDS

Part of the English legal system of land ownership, whether purchasing or selling, is to have a document, or a deed, that attests to the transaction. From early settlement, the English constantly pressured the sachems to "sell" them land.

In the early days, Wampanoag people felt they were granting the English the right to use the land as we would use it, but that would not prevent us from continuing to use it as we always had.

Indigenous people did not have the concept of "buying" and "selling" land. We did have ways and customs regarding the use of land, and the acknowledgment of boundaries. We believed that only the Creator who made the land could own it. We cannot sell what does not belong to us.

This is another process that caused a lot of contention, misunderstanding, and mistrust between English and Indigenous people. When the English signed a deed, they believed they owned that land exclusively. They did not want other English, even, or Indigenous people to cross it, farm it, forage it, or hunt on it, even if that is what Indigenous people had been doing for centuries. These were times the English did build fences and made sure the gates were locked.

By the mid-1700s, Indigenous people realized they could be separated from land. They, too, began to utilize the paper deeds, as they became a way to at least try to hold on to certain lands, which, of course, people needed to support themselves and their families. People continued to hunt, fish, farm, forage, and carry out many traditional ways and practices. Having the land to do that is key to the continuation of culture. So people wrote deeds and registered them with the English courts, hoping that they and their children and grandchildren would have places to live, presently and in the future.

THE ENGLISH DON'T MAKE IT EASY

In 1661, a man named Daniel Gookin became the Superintendent of the Praying Indians (more on them later on). He traveled to the various Indigenous communities, assessed the conditions of the people living there, and reported on this in several volumes. One was *Historical Collections of the Indians of New England* in 1674. Here is an excerpt from the book, regarding Indigenous lands.

If any should object, that it is not necessary, that the English should grant them land, forasmuch as it was all their native country and propriety, before the English came into America; the answer is ready: First, that the English claim right to their land, by patent from our king. Secondly, yet the English had the grant of most of the land within this jurisdiction, either by purchase or donation from the Indian sachems and sagamores, which were actually in possession, when the English came first over. Therefore the propriety is in the English; and it is necessary for the Indians, as the case stands, for their present and future security and tranquility, to receive the lands by grant from the English, who are a growing and potent people, comparatively to the Indians.

Let's take a critical look at this paragraph. The English "assumed ownership" of the entire continent, as described in their land patent. And now, fifty years after first settlement, they have possession of enough land to grant it back to Indigenous people. Now they're actually going to discuss whether it is *necessary* for Indigenous people to have any land? Whether Indigenous people have a place to live in their own homelands?

They did recognize that this all was Indigenous land: "forasmuch as it was all their native country and propriety . . ." But that had changed now, because "the English claim right to their land, by patent from [the English] king."

Review the section on the land patents, which talks about the size of the territory they claim. The patents use words like "from sea to sea" with graphic descriptions of every river, lake, inlet, stream, and hill in between.

The King of England, with help from the Doctrine of Discovery, created a legal right to all the countries and lands he was claiming. But did he have a moral or ethical right to do this? Is there equality in these actions? Is there respect for different people and their ways of life?

Further, "the English had the grant of most of the land within this jurisdiction, either by purchase or donation from the Indian sachems and sagamores . . ." Note the key words here: "purchase or donation." "Purchase" usually involves a deed, whereas a "donation" is a gift. These were rarely simple, straightforward transitions of land from one party to another. Land transactions often involved coercion, deception, or even outright swindling, with such "purchases" or "donations" not being appropriately represented in a deed. If the English couldn't find a willing sachem, or if there was not one (remember, this is post-plague and the tribal nations were still trying to regain some semblance of normalcy), the English would find any likely, even random, Indigenous person to sign a deed. It sometimes occurred that a single Native person from one tribal nation or community would "sell" land for other, or even several, communities. Even though these individuals were under pressure from colonial authorities, such actions are the complete opposite of traditional ways of passing land use rights within a community.

Deeds were written by an English person, who signed

all the signatures, as many Indigenous people were not reading or writing at this time, making their "mark" on documents instead. They likely were not fluent in the English language—and the English did not speak the Wampanoag language. There is cause to doubt whether some interpreters, English or Indigenous, honestly translated exactly what was written in the deeds.

And finally,

Therefore the property is in the English; and it is necessary for the English, as the case stands, for their present and future security and tranquility . . .

The "security and tranquility" of Indigenous people comes from our land, our ways of life on the land, and our relationship to it. The English cannot give us those things, particularly as they relentlessly pressured sachems for ever more land.

The more land we don't have, the more potential to lose ourselves, our cultural ways, our spiritual ways. Our language, which is thousands and thousands of years old, reflected that we could not be separated from our land—that we and the land are one thing. Everything from our entire traditional lives came from the land: our food, cultivated, foraged, hunted, or fished; our clothing from animal hides and plant fibers; our medicines from the plants and animals;

our houses from the trees and marsh reeds; and fire to cook our food, heat our homes, make our tools and boats, and conduct ceremony. The responsibility of humans, in return, is to keep the earth as created; to keep all of Creator's systems of life working as created; to keep the balance of life.

How are we secure and tranquil when the ability to do all these things has been stopped?

RELIGIOUS FREEDOM, RELIGIOUS CONVERSION

Another process of colonization was the effort to convert Indigenous people to Christianity. While the Pilgrims themselves were not missionaries who arrived with the intention to convert Indigenous people, they certainly had the thought.

In *Mourt's Relation: A Journal of the Pilgrims at Plimoth,* written in 1622, the statements appear: "They [Indigenous people] are a people without any religion or knowledge of any God. . . ." And that the English did have the intention of "carrying the Gospel of Christ into those foreign parts, amongst those people that as yet have had no knowledge nor taste of God . . ."

These are *assumptions* that the Pilgrims made about Wampanoag people. The English never considered that Wampanoag "religion" or spiritual practices and beliefs were valid ways of prayer and ceremony. Instead, they acted on their assumptions as if they were truth.

The success of Plimoth Colony on Wampanoag land opened the floodgates for other Europeans to come here and create other colonies. With more settlers came the missionaries, and religious conversion efforts began in full force. By 1640, Thomas Mayhew arrived on the island of Capawack, or Martha's Vineyard. There were four Wampanoag villages on the island: Takemmy, Nunnepog, Chappaquiddick, and Aquinnah. Mayhew "purchased" the entire island from the Governor of New York. *How could either of these men "purchase" or "sell" land, having no previous connection with, or not involve, the island sachems in their transactions?* Clearly, they were acting on the concepts of the Doctrine of Discovery. Almost two hundred years after the papal bulls were issued by the Pope, they were firmly embedded in the minds of European people.

The first Indigenous convert in this area of southern New England was in 1643, a man named Hiacoomes from the Chappaquiddick tribe. He seemed to willingly, without question, embrace Christianity. He later became a minister himself and preached to other Indigenous people.

One tactic that the English used to Christianize Indigenous people was attempting to convert the sachems and other community leaders, thinking that their people would simply follow along. Many Indigenous people did accept Christianity, but many did not, and it was a divisive force within Native communities. A primary reason for its acceptance was the aftermath of the Great Dying, as people were in such great psychological, emotional, and spiritual turmoil because of the devastation of the plague, which nothing in our ancient cultures could stop. This is perhaps why Hiacoomes and others could accept Christianity.

The English perceived Christian Indigenous people as the "good Indians," and those who wanted to live traditionally as the "bad Indians." The pressure to convert was so great that it was literally a matter of life and death. Convert or die.

Another excerpt from Gookin's *Historical Collections* is a report on the conditions of Indigenous people in southern New England at the time. In the chapter "Of the other Means and Instruments,

The Old Indian Meetinghouse in the Mashpee Wampanoag community, built in 1684, is still used today for ceremonies, weddings, and funerals.

used and improved for Civilizing and reducing the Indians from Barbarism," Gookin says the following about Native people:

> *Forasmuch as a pious magistracy and christian government is a great help and means for promoting, cherishing, encouraging, and propagating, the christian religion among any people, especially a nation so circumstanced, as these rude, uncultivated, and barbarous Indians were; care was taken by the general court of the Massachusetts, at the motion of Mr. Eliot, to appoint some of the most prudent and pious Indians, in every Indian village that had received the gospel, to be rulers and magistrates among them, to order their affairs both civil and criminal, and of a more ordinary and inferiour nature. These rulers were chosen by themselves, but approved by a superiour authority.*

Daniel Gookin here bluntly communicates his, and the generally held, opinion of Indigenous people: rude, uncultivated, barbarous, and needing approval by a superior authority. Regardless of the efforts to Christianize them, or their acceptance of it, Indigenous people continued to be viewed as less than human.

PRAYING TOWNS

Part of the colonial restructuring process utilizing Christianity was the creation of Praying Towns by Massachusetts Bay Colony in 1646. The Reverend John Eliot of Newton, Massachusetts, established more than twenty among the Wampanoag and Nipmuc people in Massachusetts, including three in Connecticut. In the Praying Towns, Indigenous people who wanted to convert lived separately from those who wished to maintain a traditional lifestyle.

In the Praying Towns, the English dictated most aspects of life. We were to live in English-style houses, wear English clothing, and not wear our hair long. We were to worship, work, and farm like the English. We should *be* like the English.

After King Philip's War in 1676, the General Court dismantled the majority of the Praying Towns. Those remaining went under colonial supervision in their respective areas. The people still living in them either died out or moved away, the land then reverting to the towns or the colony.

The town of West Tisbury on Martha's Vineyard had previously been part of the Wampanoag village of Takemmy. In 1659, the sachem, Josiah, set aside one square mile to become Christiantown

This little chapel was built in 1828 in Christiantown, and still stands today next to the ancient cemetery. After King Philip's War, the Praying Towns were no longer overseen by the colonial government, although people continued to live in these communities. Families lived in Christiantown into the early twentieth century.

for those Wampanoag people who chose to convert to Christianity, or determined it was the best way to survive.

Although Christiantown had not been a legal Praying Town for more than two hundred years, Wampanoag people continued to live there into the early twentieth century. This author's great-grandfather was born there. The once–square mile tract has since been divided, with the Martha's Vineyard Land Bank owning most of it. The remaining portion belongs to the Wampanoag Tribe of Gay Head (Aquinnah). There is a tiny chapel where Thomas Mayhew, the missionary who "purchased" Martha's Vineyard, preached to Wampanoag people. Across the road on the hillside is an ancient cemetery. Even though people had converted to Christianity, they still followed traditional burial practices. All but one or two of the graves have a large rock at the head, and a smaller rock at the foot about four feet away. The graves are short because people were buried in the fetal position, like babies in their mother's womb. All the headstones face toward the southwest, and people are born back into the home of the Creator when they die.

KING PHILIP'S WAR, 1675

The man known as King Philip was the son of Massasoit, the Pokanoket Wampanoag leader known for negotiating an alliance of mutual protection with the Pilgrims in March of 1621. This agreement remained in place throughout Massasoit's life. When he passed away in 1660, his older son, Wamsutta, became sachem. Wamsutta died very shortly thereafter under suspicious circumstances. Wampanoag people felt he had been poisoned by the English.

Undermining, or even killing, Indigenous leadership was yet another method of colonization. By this point in time, a number of Wampanoag leaders had been targeted as a threat to Plimoth Colony and had been killed as criminals. The colonial government continued to assert its authority over that of the sachems, rendering them powerless to act in defense of their people or lands.

Upon Wamsutta's death, his younger brother Pometacom, also called Philip, became sachem. He realized that negotiating with the English for any sort of reasonable agreement was not going to happen. Throughout the region, the ability of Indigenous people to maintain any semblance of our traditional lives was constantly encroached upon. Philip recognized that Indigenous people were losing our homelands and ancient ways of life. That is what had been steadily happening since 1620. After fifty-five years of "negotiation" that always favored the English, in 1675 he concluded there was no resolution but war.

Philip traveled to the various Wampanoag communities, including those on Martha's Vineyard and Nantucket. He went to the Narragansett, Nipmuc, Mohegan, Pequot, Niantic, and as far as Mohawk country in what is now New York State, trying to gather as many people as possible to push the English back across the water. Many did join Pometacom, and Indigenous people had the advantage for a while. They burned and leveled twelve English towns and were successful in many skirmishes out in the forests. The turning point came when the English began to learn Indigenous fighting methods. This gave them the upper hand, as they had more people to be soldiers. King Philip's War ended when he was shot and killed on August 12, 1676. We estimate he was only about thirty-five years old. He is still much loved and highly respected among Wampanoag people today for his valiant efforts to save our lands and traditional ways.

After the war, life dramatically worsened for all Indigenous people in the region. Boatloads of men from all the tribes in southern New England were shipped out of the country and sold into slavery in the Caribbean islands. Men from Wampanoag, Narragansett, Nipmuc, Mohegan, Pequot, and Niantic were taken away for the express purpose of getting them so far away there was no possibility of ever returning home. The people left behind would no longer have the ability to resist English encroachment. Their lives were completely subjected to colonial domination.

RESERVATIONS, INDIAN DISTRICTS, LAND ALLOTMENTS

As early as 1665, Indian Districts began to be established. "District" is a fancy way of saying "reservation," before that term came into broader use in the 1800s with Indigenous people in the western part of the country.

Two of these districts encompassed the original villages of Aquinnah and Mashpee. On Martha's Vineyard, most people from the four Wampanoag villages were moved into Aquinnah; people from villages on Cape Cod were moved into Mashpee. Districts or reservations were where Indigenous people were put to remove them from the land that other people wanted. They were put onto land that was undesirable (at least at that moment in time).

The reservations had white overseers, as it was felt that Indigenous people were not capable of handling their own affairs. Within reservations were areas that were tribally or communally owned. Other lands were given out in allotments, which might be, for example, sixty acres, to individual families. This introduced the concept of "private property" and is a practice that completely interrupted traditional land use and care practices. It did not eliminate them, but it did change how they were carried out.

Indigenous people living in these districts or reservations were wards of the state, once Massachusetts became a state in 1788. "Ward" is the term applied to those considered not able to handle their own affairs and needing state supervision to function. The allotment lands in Mashpee and Aquinnah were inalienable, meaning they could not be taken away from Wampanoag people. This was stated in the documents that established the allotment system.

That sounded really good . . . for a minute anyway. In 1869, Massachusetts apparently changed its mind about the ward situation, and made Wampanoag people state citizens! Could this actually be a step toward equality? That's a nice thought, but not one that reflected reality. The state also lifted the restraints regarding the land being inalienable to us. In 1870, largely against the wishes

This map shows the Town of Mashpee in 1877 when the land was divided into parcels that were allotted to each Wampanoag family, or for other uses. This is essentially the opposite of our traditional land use practices.

of Wampanoag people, the state abolished the district status, and made both Aquinnah and Mashpee towns. These changes were not in the interest of Wampanoag people trying to preserve homelands and culture. This was not a step toward equality, because in a town, the land is opened up, and anyone can come in to buy and sell "property."

ERASURE BY RENAMING

Maps and mapping are yet other processes that have removed Indigenous people from the landscape. From the 1600s on, many Europeans who came here drew maps of the locales and regions that they traveled to. They sometimes did obtain and use the names of various places or features on the land from Indigenous people. Sometimes they didn't ask or just didn't use Indigenous names for the village areas, rivers, lakes and ponds, the ocean, or the forests or meadows. They renamed places after themselves, someone in their family, country, or leadership, thereby eliminating Indigenous names—and presence.

As more and more maps were made, fewer and fewer original Indigenous names were used. When they do appear, the spelling is often so corrupted from the Wampanoag language that the words cannot be translated. The name might also have no relevance to the place named—it is just the use of the word.

Indigenous names are hugely informational in themselves. The languages are very descriptive and can provide pictures of what the landscape used to look like. The word "Aquinnah" (aqunah) means "the end of the land," and refers to the cliffs that meet the ocean. "Mashpee" (maseepee) means "big water," and refers to Mashpee Pond, the largest body on inland water on Cape Cod.

The landscape has completely changed from the 1600s when just Indigenous people lived here, due to deforestation, damming of rivers, housing, and business and industry development. All of these things overlay and destroy the landscape that Indigenous people have lived with and cared for for millennia.

LET'S THINK ABOUT THIS:

1. Compared with "When Life Was Our Own," how did the land allotment system interrupt traditional land use practices?

2. Compare this process of dispossession to the definition of racism at the beginning of the book.

3. How would history be different if the English had not made so many assumptions about Indigenous people, and had really taken the time to speak with us about our cultural and spiritual ways? How are these assumptions contradicted in "When Life Was Our Own"? Find one way in each season.

CHAPTER 9

WHEN LIFE WAS OUR OWN: AUTUMN— TROUBLE LOOMS

Over the summer, word was getting around that people from the villages of Big Rock and Deep Water had things go missing from their homes at the planting sites. Different furs had disappeared, as well as dried food preserved for winter. This situation all came to a head with a third theft just as the harvest season was beginning.

A young man named Beaver Tail had been seen leaving the home of another person from the same village of Big Rock. He carried a large gray wolf skin, rolled up under his arm so as to conceal it. He had entered the home when no one was there and rifled through their belongings to find the hide.

The family who had been robbed went to the sachem of their village, Breath of Wind, telling him of this crime. Breath of Wind called his council together to discuss the matter, and Beaver Tail was brought before them. Many people from several villages had gathered to hear what would become of this young man. It was not a usual thing to have such a crime committed. People highly valued their relationships within their communities, and this was a primary way order was kept. Everyone understood that harmony, and not discord, must be maintained for life and living to be in balance. Stealing, therefore, was akin to murder, as it was such an affront, such an act of complete disrespect.

Sachem Breath of Wind heard the complaint of the family whose wolf skin was taken. They were extremely upset at having been treated this way. The sachem and council also listened to Beaver Tail, who said he took the skin because his mother had no furs to keep her warm. They had no other family members to provide for them.

Sachem Breath of Wind and the council knew that Beaver Tail was guilty, as several people had seen him carrying away the wolf skin. They were also aware that his mother did have other furs for her comfort—so Beaver Tail had not only stolen but had lied as well.

Breath of Wind sharply reprimanded Beaver Tail in front of all who were there, and he had him return the wolf skin. That was the punishment, since Beaver Tail had never done anything like this before. Everyone thought that would be the end of it, because Beaver Tail had been embarrassed in front of the entire community by the sachem. That would be enough to deter most people from committing such an act.

However, it wasn't long before someone from the Deep Water community came back to their house to find a bobcat skin, two red fox skins, and two beaver skins missing. It was obvious that someone had plundered their belongings to find them.

Another person from Deep Water saw Beaver Tail and recognized him as the thief from Big Rock. He had been there the day of Beaver Tail's reprimand.

Upon hearing of this unwanted visitor, Sachem Owl Feather of Deep Water sent a runner to Breath of Wind. When the runner, Thunder Caller, arrived, he was invited into Breath of Wind's house. They smoked the pipe, as was the custom, and had some food. Afterward, he delivered the message that Beaver Tail had been seen in their community, walking away with a bundle under his arm.

Men from Deep Water escorted Beaver Tail back to Big Rock, where once again he was brought before Breath of Wind and the council. This time there was no question of his guilt and no discussion needed. The punishment was clear. This second offense brought Beaver Tail another public rebuke from Breath of Wind, and a beating on his back with a stick.

The pain of the beating and the public humiliation were usually more than enough to stanch the unwanted behavior, and have the perpetrator change his ways. Unfortunately, this was not the case with Beaver Tail.

He committed a third offense, going into the home of a family in Little Bird's community of Green Pine. Beaver Tail robbed an older woman and her husband, Mist at Dawn and Stone Walker. They had recently lost their only son, who had provided them with meat and furs. Since his death, they relied on their daughter's husband and his brothers.

Beaver Tail took two baskets of smoked shellfish, part of the family's winter food, and a large bear skin from the bed. As it happened, Grandpa Rabbit saw Beaver Tail emerging from the home just before sunset when he thought he wouldn't be seen. Mist at Dawn and Stone Walker were off visiting another family and having dinner.

Grandpa Rabbit called out, and Strong Bear, Tall Pine, and Walks in the Moonlight came running. They found Beaver Tail just about to slip away into the woods. They brought him to their sachem, Corn Tassel. She sent a runner to Breath of Wind. In the meantime, Beaver Tail was escorted, for the third time, and brought before Breath of Wind and the Big Rock council.

It was an extremely rare occurrence to have a third offense committed. Again, the punishment was clear. Breath of Wind slit the end of Beaver Tail's nose with a knife, which would leave a permanent scar on his face. The scar would tell everyone he met of the crimes he had committed, and he would be shunned.

Because Beaver Tail had caused so much disruption in three different communities, Breath of Wind and the council discussed banishing him from the village, to never be allowed to return. One council person suggested that the people he had stolen from have the choice to simply banish him or to kill him, as his crimes were so egregious. Everyone agreed to offer this choice to the families.

The three families met with Breath of Wind and the Big Rock council and discussed what should be done with Beaver Tail. Some did not feel confident he wouldn't steal again, given his past brazen behavior and disrespect.

Beaver Tail's mother, Wood Violet, came to Breath of Wind and pleaded for her son's life. She was old now, and he was her main support. He did provide her with meat and fish. She begged Breath of Wind not to banish or to kill him. But she could not promise that her son would not steal again.

The families, Breath of Wind, and the council discussed all of this at length, but could come to no consensus. Finally, one council person suggested they talk to Sachems Corn Tassel from Green Pine and Owl Feather from Deep Water about joining people from Big Rock in a game of football.

The game was not played for entertainment but used to resolve issues such as this. The game would determine Beaver Tail's fate: whether he would live but be banished forever, or whether he would die.

Men from Big Rock formed a team to play against an equal number of men from Green Pine and Deep Water. Football was played on beaches with firm sand, where the tide went way, way out.

The men set up two goalposts about one mile up the beach from each other. Strong Bear made a new ball, about the size of a pattypan squash, just a bit too big to fit in your hand. The ball was made of deerskin and stuffed with deer hair. Strong Bear finished it with a painted red, black, and yellow design.

It was decided if the Big Rock team won, Beaver Tail would live but be banished. If the Green Pine/ Deep Water team won, then he would be killed.

The game started about midmorning the next day. All in all, there were about a hundred people on each team. Only one goal was required for the win, due to the distance between the goals.

The Big Rock team painted their faces red with a wide black stripe down the middle from hairline to chin. The Green Pine/Deep Water team's faces were white with a thin black line across the cheeks and noses.

The game started at a point halfway between the goalposts. Breath of Wind threw the ball into the air between the two teams and the game was on! People from all the communities lined the beach, back up along the bank, out of the way of the players to watch the game and cheer the teams on. Farther down the beach, some of the women set up cook fires and prepared food. The game could go on all day, or it might have to stop at dusk and resume the next day if no goal had been made.

The teams played well into the afternoon, stopping for a break every now and then. Sometimes it seemed

...ame was working itself closer to one goalpost, ...o have the ball played way in the direction of the ... Players could throw, kick, or run and carry the ...aking the chance of being tackled by people on ...her team.

...nally, just as the sun was beginning to set, the ...ng goal was made! The game had worked its ...oward the Big Rock goalpost, where one player ...d the ball and gave it a strong, hefty kick across ...oal!

...nd so it was that Beaver Tail would live. But he ...o pack all his belongings and get ready to leave ...ome. Wherever he went in the world, people

*Games such as football were often
used to resolve conflicts,
rather than fighting or war.*

would know of his crimes because of the scar on his nose. He held his mother in a tight hug before turning and walking away. Wood Violet broke down in a torrent of tears, collapsing on the ground. Breath of Wind and his wife went to her and helped her get up and into her house. They made her some fresh mint tea and stayed and talked with her for a long while. They reassured her that she would be cared for. Breath of Wind and his family would provide her with corn and vegetables as she needed, and his sons and brothers would bring her meat and furs and fish.

Wood Violet began to compose herself. She knew the right decision had been made about her son. She already missed him terribly! It tore her heart to lose him, but she knew she could carry on with her life. The communities of Big Rock, Deep Water, and Green Pine could now ease their minds and look forward to the rest of the harvest.

CHAPTER 10

LAWS: THE EUROPEAN LEGAL SYSTEM IMPOSED

WAMPANOAG LAW

The Europeans assumed that the "Eden" they found when they arrived (see Chapter 4) happened randomly or naturally, on its own, with no human intervention. They assumed that Indigenous people were "rude, uncultivated, barbarous," with "no art, science, skill or faculty" to do anything with the land. We've seen from passages in other sections, in the quotes from *Mourt's Relation* and Gookin's *Historical Collections,* that Europeans considered Indigenous people to be without laws or social order. These are assumptions, instruments of colonization used to justify the taking of land.

Of course, Indigenous people had and have systems to keep people accountable and acting in accordance with the structure of their society! We built our lives and cultures around the ways that Creator put into place to make everything work in balance. At the time of Creation, everyone, everything, was given a job. Humans were to maintain the earth as created, to keep the balance that Creator put into place. We observed everything Creator made and developed our cultural values from that.

Within traditional societies, thinking, attitudes, behaviors, and actions were developed through the social structure of the people, which was built on the foundation of the values. People were raised with respect, seeing respect showed not just to other people, but to everything in Creation. When you have respect, it develops humility. This means that you (as an individual, family, race, society) have the ability to let others be who they are. The need is not in you to assert dominance, authority, or personality over others in order for you to feel right or in control.

In everyday life, children were raised by these values into respectful and humble adults. This was inherent in them. This isn't to say that Indigenous people didn't have issues and problems, that they didn't mess up or have accidents, that they didn't hurt somebody else's feelings, or that they weren't stubborn. Indigenous people are human beings just like other people. But the *system* of values that guided Indigenous societies kept people living in right relationship (honoring Creator's plan). The evidence is the "Eden" that the early Europeans saw: The earth and natural processes were working right because people were living right.

Humor, teasing, and laughter are other ways the norms of Indigenous society were "enforced." They are still a huge part of Indigenous cultures. Always, every day! If someone has made some sort of misstep, family and friends will be sure to indulge in some teasing. This is not done to make someone feel bad, but it may be to make a point, or to bring a laugh. People have been known to reach the age of eighty-five and still get teased or called a nickname for something they did when they were seven. Remember in "When Life Was Our Own" how Strawberry chipmunked out with the strawberry picking, "putting away" more than she gathered for her family? How was she taught about her behavior? With gentle teasing and no shame, her family communicated how she should be thinking as she went out to gather, not just about strawberries but anything.

Indigenous people have relationship with the land, working with natural systems to keep them as created or enhance them. Everything flourished, greatly benefiting the people and the land. These practices of relationship were developed over centuries, whether for food, housing, clothing, medicine, fire, or weather protection. By the time of the arrival of the Europeans in the 1600s, these practices had been in use for thousands of years. This "managed" landscape is what Europeans saw and called "Eden." These practices were all based on the values that are part of Indigenous societies that begin with respect and humility. Can you find another example of living in right relationship in "When Life Was Our Own"?

For example, we didn't pollute any body of water. Creator made the waters and gifted them to us. As such, we humble ourselves to honor that creation, and we give thanks for that which allows us to continue our lives. We understood that the waters are all connected to one another, and to everything in Creation. All of Creation is largely made of water. Our relatives, whether plant, animal, mineral, or earth, depend on water, whether it or the land is their home. Water has the right to be as it was created, as does everything in Creation. Everything in Creation is to be kept as Creator intended. We do not destroy that which Creator has made. This is following natural law. So we didn't put chemicals into the waters that the fish ingest, that the eagles and bears then eat and become sick and die. If all this happens to our relatives (fish, eagles, bears), then it happens to us.

In traditional times, each of the Wampanoag villages was autonomous, having its own sachem or chief. Within the villages, the sachems and councils made decisions about the use of the land: where the winter villages would be built, where the summer planting fields would be, who lived in them, and which would lie fallow. Sachems routinely negotiated with each other if any certain land area was to be shared for any purpose.

Sachems of any number of villages might join in a confederation to address any sort of issue that arose. The confederation could be two, ten, or all sixty-nine villages, depending on the matter at hand. These alliances usually dissolved once the situation had been resolved.

In the summer homes, the women were in charge of the land, both the garden areas and the households. They were the main planters and tenders of the gardens, being akin to the corn as both are female spirits. People recognized that everything Creator made is alive and has spirit. Men and women followed the guidance of that kinship in everything they did. Women were the mothers and the caretakers of the homes, doing the cooking, cleaning, hide tanning, or medicine preparation. They sewed clothing and made many of the household things the family used every day. They took care of the kids, the elders, and those who were sick or injured.

People traveled all the time between villages, and

often had relatives, in-laws, cousins, and friends all over. In formal situations, there was protocol upon entering the territory of another sachem, which was to go to his or her home first. He or she, any councilors, and the guests would first smoke the pipe, guests would be offered food, and then they would discuss the business at hand.

Sachems were not monarchs who ruled over people, telling everybody what to do. They came to their positions based on the strength of their character, their integrity, honesty, and the love, care, and respect they showed for their people. It was the sachem's, and his family's, responsibility to care for and provide for those in need. They didn't "rule," but worked with the clan mothers, elders, and warrior councils to make the best decisions for the well-being of their entire community.

Wampanoag traditional culture, like many other Indigenous societies, did not have a huge body of laws designed to control people. We did not have police, courts, or judges. We did not have these things because we did not need them.

In traditional times, there were very few criminals because we had very few crimes. People were free to act and think as they saw fit, as long as no harm was brought to anyone or anything. Thought and action were formed on the framework of the values. This means that while people had freedom, it came with responsibility. There was consequence to actions, so thought was given to how other beings would be affected, as everything in Creation is related. Any issues or offenses were usually handled between the individuals or the families involved. If this did not happen, they could go to their sachem or medicine people to help with resolution of the problem.

In Wampanoag traditional society, there were three primary, extremely egregious, crimes: stealing, lying, and murder. Lying was akin to stealing, as it is so horribly disrespectful. Like stealing, it is taking something from someone—their dignity as a human being. If you can lie to someone, you have no respect for them as a person. Being truthful is a form of respect.

Murder, of course, was and is the worst that anyone can do to another human—to make the decision to end the life of another person. Even if the death was something that was not planned, the one who took the life is still responsible for that life.

In traditional times, when a murder was committed among Wampanoag people, the family of the victim had several choices, which they could work through with their sachem. They could kill the murderer, they could choose to banish the murderer, or they could accept an offering of wampum. Wampum is beads made from the shell of the quahog, a hard-shell saltwater clam, which is white on the inside with a rim of purple. The beads were woven into belts, which were not meant to be worn, but were created for many different

Wampum belts are still made and used just as they were hundreds of years ago. This Wampum belt was made in 2020 and relates to the story of healing after colonization. It is four and a half feet long and nine inches wide.

purposes, like treaty agreements or condolence, and are highly valued. The choice of which of the three options depended on the nature of the crime. In Wampanoag society, the outcome was determined relatively speedily. There were no long trials that could go on for years, no loopholes for perpetrators to slip through to avoid consequences, no juggling of legalities that can veil or shield the crime. The process was comparatively direct, simple, straightforward, and fast. Closure was brought to the family, the crime was resolved, grieving could begin and go through its process—sorrow, heartache, missing the person—so the lives of the living could better resume normalcy, or balance.

In "When Life Was Our Own," look at all the care, prayer, ceremony, and thanksgiving that went into picking strawberries, catching a fish, hunting a deer or a turkey, picking herbs for medicine, or cutting down a tree for a boat. Those are all life-ending activities. It does not matter that they are not human lives. They were lives given by the Creator, and each being in Creation has the right to live out its own life. All beings in Creation depend on the lives of others so that theirs can continue. Bears have to eat. Whales have to eat. Mice have to eat. Trees have to "eat." Daisies have to eat. People have to eat. That is the cycle of life Creator made. When living in right relationship, following natural law, we do not forget our responsibility in the taking of any life. That is not done without consequence and we don't just destroy that which Creator has made. Creator instructed us in prayer, thanksgiving, and ceremony to respect the lives of those we take to ensure our own continue. This is the purposeful, intentional thinking, acting, and behaving, following practices that support our lives while nurturing, nourishing, and enhancing the earth. That makes the balance of Creation.

ENGLISH LAW AND THE BEGINNINGS OF AMERICAN LAW

We've talked earlier about the Pilgrims landing north of "Virginia" at Cape Cod, and creating the Mayflower

Compact as a working document to cover themselves, since they were out of English "jurisdiction." They established Plimoth Colony in 1620, with a charter, or land patent, from the King of England. This was done with no consultation or negotiation with Wampanoag leaders, whose territory was being claimed. Massachusetts Bay Colony was established in 1630, with more English people pouring into the Boston area. In 1692, Plimoth Colony ended, being absorbed into Massachusetts Bay Colony.

THE

COLONIAL LAWS

OF

MASSACHUSETTS.

REPRINTED FROM THE EDITION OF
1 6 6 0,
WITH THE SUPPLEMENTS TO 1672.

CONTAINING ALSO,

THE BODY OF LIBERTIES OF
1641.

PUBLISHED BY ORDER OF THE CITY COUNCIL OF BOSTON, UNDER
THE SUPERVISION OF WILLIAM H. WHITMORE,
RECORD COMMISSIONER.

WITH A COMPLETE INDEX.

Rothman&Co.
Littleton, Colorado
1995

The title page of
The Colonial Laws of Massachusetts.
These laws were designed to control every aspect of Indigenous people's lives.

By 1660—just forty years after the Pilgrims settled—the English had developed a complete volume of laws: *The Colonial Laws of Massachusetts.* Entire sections contained laws to govern Indigenous people. In 1674, Daniel Gookin in his *Historical Collections* discusses these laws, which clearly describe the situation Indigenous people were living in:

> *There are diverse other laws and orders, made by the general court of Massachusetts, relating unto the Indians,*

which are printed and published . . . in order to their good . . . giving instructions and directions, backed with penalties, for promoting and practicing morality, civility, industry, and diligence in their particular callings: for idleness and improvidence are the Indians' greatest sin, and in a kind of second nature to them, which by good example and wholesome laws, gradually applied, with God's blessing, may be rooted out.

Each section below explores pieces excerpted from *The Colonial Laws of Massachusetts.*

I. "DECLARING THE INDIANS' TITLE TO LANDS . . ."

By 1660, the English had acquired all or most of Indigenous lands, and were now in a position to grant title to Indigenous people for their own ancient homelands. How did such a complete reversal of "ownership" occur?

The epidemics that occurred throughout the 1600s played a huge part in opening up land. Even though so many died in the Great Dying or subsequent epidemics, the people remaining did not give up their country. A common misunderstanding today is: "Well, they all died and didn't need the land anymore." Think of it this way: Suppose disease killed five hundred thousand people in Boston. Could people from Greece just drop in and claim the city as now belonging to Greece?

Why not?

Because Boston is part of the state of Massachusetts, one of the fifty states in the United States. Boston would still have people and community and governmental structure that would be functional and operational.

And that is exactly how it was with the Wampanoag and other Indigenous nations. The English knew this, but still assumed they had the right to colonize. The Doctrine of Discovery is still very evident in these actions.

2. "THE CIVIL INDIANS TO HAVE LANDS GRANTED THEM FOR TOWNS."

"Civil" here means those Indigenous people who adopted Christianity, and tried to live and become like the English. Only those who had given up traditional ways, in other words, could be awarded land for towns.

People were being forced to convert to Christianity upon penalty of death. They perhaps didn't believe in Christianity in their hearts and didn't want to reject traditional life. But it became a matter of life and death. The "civil Indians" were the "good Indians," and those who chose to continue traditional ways were the "bad" ones. Adopting Christianity became a matter of survival.

As mentioned, Wampanoag people had sixty-nine towns prior to European settlement. Even after the Great Dying, many of these original communities still existed at this midpoint in the seventeenth century, or at least families that remained in the territory of their village. Some had become Praying Towns, but nevertheless, people continued living as Wampanoag people because that's who they were. The same was true for all other Indigenous people in the state and in southern New England.

3. "INDIANS NOT TO BE DISPOSSESSED OF WHAT LANDS THEY HAVE SUBDUED, OR FROM THEIR FISHING PLACES . . ."

Subdued. "Subdue" here means to farm or cultivate. Words in the seventeenth century sometimes had very different usage from that of today. Back then, subdue also meant to bring into subjection; conquer, vanquish, or to overcome, as by persuasion or training; control.

Land, therefore, is something to be conquered; put into subjection; vanquished; controlled. This is the "civil" thing to do, that which "civil" people do. Wampanoag and other Indigenous people were expected to "subdue" the land like the English, to treat it, use it, farm it as they did.

4. "NONE TO BUY LANDS FROM THE INDIANS WITHOUT LICENSE OF THE COURT."

Read this one carefully; it has a bit of a twist in it.

And it is so ordered, That no person whatsoever, shall henceforth buy Land of any Indian without License first had and obtained of the General Court; and if any offend herein, such Land so bought shall be forfeited to the Country.

At first this sounds pretty good, like it has the intent to protect Indigenous people against fraud in the sale of land. But look closely. Who is this law protecting?

If a non-Native person fails to get the proper license, you would think, logically, that the sale would be null and void, and the land would remain with the Indigenous person. But this law does not say that. It says if there is no license, then the land will be "forfeited to the Country." "The Country"? That would be America, or more specifically the colonial government in Boston. The English developed many such "methods" to obtain Indigenous lands.

5. "ALL STRONG LIQUORS PROHIBITED TO BE SOLD OR GIVEN TO THE INDIANS . . . UNLESS IN CASE OF SICKNESS, BY PERMISSION."

We had no intoxicating drinks or substances in our traditional culture. Alcohol and liquors were brought over and introduced to Indigenous people by the English. But by the 1660s, apparently, drinking among Indigenous people had become enough of an issue to need laws regarding it.

"Permission" was needed when the English or later the Americans wanted land deeds or other documents signed by Indigenous people, who might not sign if their minds weren't taken away by being under the influence. Interesting that such manipulation became law.

6. "POWWOWS, AND WIZARDS AND WITCHES, PROHIBITED UPON PENALTY."

The word "powwow" is actually a corruption of the Wampanoag word for "healer," one who heals. This is what we called our medicine people, because that is what they did. They healed people of physical problems and mental, emotional, or spiritual problems. Healing brought balance back into people's lives.

Another tool of colonization was demonizing aspects of our traditional culture. Those others depended on heavily—our healers—were demonized by being called witches, wizards, and sorcerers. The home of our ancestor Moshop on the Aquinnah cliffs was called "Devil's Den"; the bridge he started to build became "Devil's Bridge." Moshop was related to the Creator and taught the people how to live on the earth—basically opposite of the concept of "devil."

These outside concepts were imposed upon Indigenous people because of the assumptions of the English people. They are false images intended to undermine and denigrate traditional cultures. They were intended to turn the minds of Indigenous people against their own traditional ways. These concepts were instilled repeatedly over generations and centuries, with both Indigenous and non-Native people as well. For example, others believed that our ceremonies are devil-worship because that is what they've always learned. But the devil is part of the Christian belief system, and does not exist in traditional Wampanoag culture, cosmology, or language. Essentially, this law says that it was illegal for Indigenous people to practice our spiritual ways, our ceremonies. Does this align with the concept of religious freedom that the Pilgrims came here for? In "When Life Was Our Own," when Eagle Heart treated Singing Wolf, was he being devil-like?

7. "ORDERS TO RESTRAIN AND PREVENT DRUNKENNESS; AND SOME OTHERS."

In spite of such a law being written, alcohol was a tool used in the "winning" of the land that became America. It was routinely used at the signing of such documents as deeds or treaties, since it lowers people's inhibitions and natural sense of self-preservation. In the Wampanoag language, the same word meaning "crazy" is used for drunkenness.

It is quite evident to see who benefits from this set of laws, regardless of Gookin's "in order to their good." These early laws clearly reflect the goals of the Doctrine of Discovery. Today, Indian Law is its own field in the broader body of United States Law. This reflects the relationships that Indigenous nations have with federal or state governments, as different from that of other racial, ethnic, or minority groups.

LET'S THINK ABOUT THIS:

1. What might it have been like if the English had acknowledged and followed Indigenous protocols upon entering their territories? How might things have turned out differently?

2. Compare descriptions of the land in "When Life Was Our Own" and in the "Wampanoag Law" section to the condition the land is in today. What has created this difference? What are some of the ways that the land has been conquered, controlled, or overcome? Have humans benefited from these processes?

3. What has been the impact of these processes on the earth, the waters, the air, plant and animal life, the natural environment? What are the consequences of destructive impacts on the natural environment? Is it possible for humans to change their thinking and develop an attitude of relationship with the land?

CHAPTER 11

WHEN LIFE WAS OUR OWN: WINTER—TIME OF THE LONG MOON

IT'S IMPORTANT TO GET ENOUGH FIBER

Grandpa Singing Wolf was well again, up and around, going about his usual routines. Grandma Yellow Sky and the entire family were greatly relieved and happy to have him back to his old self. So Grandma decided that she could take the girls out to gather milkweed and dogbane. The Moon of Thin Ice was traveling fast into the Beaver Catching Moon, and they would have to collect the dry stalks before they began to decay.

So Yellow Sky, Little Bird, Strawberry, and

Punkinseed, along with Stands Strong, headed out toward the meadows and fields to collect both plants. Even though they were dead now, having lived their season, everyone still offered prayers and thanksgiving, because even in their death, they were still giving to the people. The women and girls would harvest as many of each plant as they could, and later, over the winter, remove the fibers from the stalks.

Milkweed grew everywhere, and the women often had a difficult time keeping it out of their cornfields. Dogbane was all over as well, but it seemed to especially like the sides of the ancient pathways that everyone used.

So Yellow Sky, Stands Strong, Blue Heron, Little Bird, Strawberry, Punkinseed, and other women from the village spent three days collecting the stalks and taking them to the storage house close to their longhouse. There was a huge pile of each type of plant by the time they were through harvesting. There's a lot of winter evenings' work, Little Bird thought, although the stories and laughter that accompanied this work were some of her favorite things!

SNOWSTORM COMING

Singing Wolf told the family that a storm was coming and they should get ready. Yellow Sky took the girls out to get wood, getting dry deadwood or dead branches from the lower parts of the trees. They stacked it under the beds, with plenty of extra in the storage house. Smiling Dove, Blue Heron, and Stands Strong made sure they had plenty of food in the house, bringing in extra from the storage pits. They had enough water for several days. The villages were always near springs, should they need to get more.

All the families in their longhouse soon had everything together. They figured the storm would hit by the following night, and they were right! Little Bird was awakened from a sound sleep by the wind howling and blowing around the house. She saw her Dad sitting up and tending the fire, as did others down the length of the house. He and the other men adjusted the smoke flaps—sheets of bark attached to poles so they could be adjusted from the ground. Just the size of the smoke holes, they were placed against the wind to keep it from blowing rain, snow, or smoke back into the house. Moments when the wind wasn't blowing so hard, the girls watched the snowflakes flying by some of them floating down past the smoke flaps, only to disappear in the rising heat of the fire.

The people had built round or rounded houses like this for hundreds of generations. The oldest, oldest ancestors had figured out that the round shape could stand strong in any wind conditions. They knew that the bulrush mats would hold the heat of the fire in, and the thick sheets of bark from huge ancient trees would protect against any rain or snowstorms. The kids were experiencing this fact of history, as everyone had a good fire going, and they were kicking off the furs that now made it too hot to sleep!

Punkinseed had slept over with Strawberry and Little Bird. They woke up in the morning to see Smiling Dove putting a kettle of water on to heat, adding some dry beans to begin cooking. She ground some corn into larger chunks, to be added to the beans when they softened. Later she would add dried blueberries to bring a little sweetness to breakfast.

FIRST SNOW

The girls got up excitedly, went to the door, and moved the hide covering aside to peek outside. In spite of all the high winds, the storm had not left a lot of snow. Little Bird had Strawberry and Punkinseed put on their boots and a fur wrap—they would step outside to greet the day. The sun was just above the horizon, a golden luminescence glowing through the snow-covered trees. The world, blanketed in white, was absolutely silent. The girls stood and listened for a few moments, hearing nothing but the deep quiet, calm, and peace that comes with new-fallen snow.

Fortunately, all the families had finished up at the summer homes and gotten back to the winter village before this early storm hit. Everyone was comfortably settling back in the longhouses, ready for winter's tasks.

ALWAYS WORK TO BE DONE

Strong Bear, Tall Pine, and Walks in the Moonlight checked all of their hunting equipment. They made new arrows, and arrowpoints of stone, antler tip and deer bone, hollow turkey or goose bone. They took some of the milkweed and dogbane stalks that had been collected and made rope for snare traps and re-pairing of dip nets. They made fishline and fishhooks for upcoming ice fishing trips to the river and ponds.

Red Dawn helped the younger boys make arrows

and points. Woodchuck was very easily learning how to knap arrowheads from the various types of stone, while River was having a harder time with this skill. He had, however, with just some basic guidance from Red Dawn and Walks in the Moonlight, made his first bow and bowstring. This would be the winter, he thought, he would get his first deer. This both excited and frightened him. He was excited because he would be bringing food to his family and making a contribution. He was frightened by the thought of actually taking a life. To see before you a living, breathing, vibrant animal living its life one minute—and lying dead and bleeding the next—was extremely daunting. Watching the life spark leave the deer's eyes, knowing there would be an empty space in the deer's family, was sad and heartbreaking. So River remembered what he had seen his Dad, Uncles, and Grandfather do all of his life—what they had done all of *their* lives—and that was the ceremonies and prayers of thanksgiving, remembering that no life should be taken in a random or destructive manner. In taking, there must be giving back. So the people lived in a way that ensured the forest home was kept as the deer needed it for their lives. Holding his finished bow in his hand, River began to fully understand the responsibility that was upon him.

As the men checked their equipment, Singing Dove, Blue Heron, and Stands Strong packed plenty of dried corn, beans, and squash, cornmeal, blueberries, and cherries, along with some walnuts and hickory nuts. They also packed a big bag of nocake, the parched cornmeal. Everyone was preparing to travel to the winter hunting lodge, where they would get deer and other smaller animals such as raccoon, beaver, and rabbit. Maybe that elk would still be in the neighborhood!

The family might be gone for a half cycle of the moon, or longer. The meat and furs would keep them through the winter. As the men hunted, the women did the skinning, then cut up the meat. Just about everything on the animal was used for some purpose, and not wasted. Wasting was not honoring the life that was just given up. Anything that could not be used was buried in a respectful way with proper ceremony.

While the others were away, Grandma Yellow Sky and Grandpa Singing Wolf would stay with Little Bird, Strawberry, and Punkinseed back in the longhouse, with the other families. Plus, there were all the other houses in the village. Most of the men also went hunting with their wives and older boys, while the elders, other women, and smaller children remained at home

STORIES IN THE TRACKS

When the family arrived at their hunting lodge, the men checked the outside bark, making sure no rain or melting snow could leak in. The women set up the inside of the house, starting a fire and tying the bulrush mats around the interior walls. Smiling Dove, Blue Heron, and Stands Strong prepared dinner. Meanwhile, Red Dawn took River and Woodchuck out to see if they could find any tracks nearby. The younger boys were trying to remember earlier lessons regarding whether a deer was male or female, how much it might weigh, whether it was calm and easy or scared and running. Red Dawn showed them other signs that deer left, if you could not see their tracks. Sometimes you had to do a little figuring, once you knew the distance from one track to the next for any particular animal. You might not see a full track or even a partial, but only a little stone misplaced to tell that someone had stepped there.

River and Woodchuck followed behind Red Dawn, heading farther into the woods. Suddenly they came upon the tracks of a deer, which were overlaid with those of a wolf. Red Dawn asked the boys to tell him what they saw happening. They observed that

Leaving tracks for the boys to read the story.

the deer was quite small. Suddenly, the deer began running. The tracks were deeper in the snow and farther apart than usual. The boys pointed out where they saw the wolf's tracks coming in from another direction. At first those tracks were purposeful and even, and then they indicated that the wolf began to run after the deer. The boys followed this story for a while, until they came to where it ended. They had come upon the place where the wolf caught the deer and killed it. The snow was all kicked up where the deer fought to escape. There were the tracks of many wolves who had come in to feed on the deer. When the boys found the remains, there was only the skeleton, some fur, and the head left.

The younger boys were very sad about the little

deer. But they already understood that in death comes life. The deer lost his life that day, but the wolves had gotten food and nourishment and their family would continue. Other animals and insects would eat the remaining scraps of meat and gnaw on the bones for their nourishment. The deer's remains would decay into the earth, enriching the soil. The boys knew that this was the cycle of life that was Creator's plan.

WINTER'S ABUNDANCE

Everyone was up early the next morning to get ready for the first hunt. After morning prayers and a good breakfast, Strong Bear, Tall Pine, Walks in the Moonlight, and Red Dawn took the little boys into the forest. They found tracks almost right away, and River and Woodchuck told the men what they saw in them. All the Dads were very pleased with how the boys were learning! The men saw a few places in their interpretation where they could have discerned more information, but basically, the boys were well on their way to becoming knowledgeable trackers.

Over the course of the day, the men got two bucks (male deer). They gutted them right away, keeping the hearts and livers, which would be eaten. They cleaned the area to be like it was before they got the deer. Tying the two front legs together and then the back, they used hefty branches to lift the deer and carry them back to the lodge. Strong Bear and Walks in the Moonlight carried one deer, and Tall Pine and Red Dawn the other, each hoisting the ends of the poles onto a shoulder. River and Woodchuck carried the packages with the hearts and livers.

When they got back to the lodge, Smiling Dove, Blue Heron, and Stands Strong already had a big pot of stew going with corn and beans. Stands Strong was pounding walnuts into flour when the men came home with the deer. Smiling Dove was making boiled bread with nocake, dried onion, and hominy pieces, forming round cakes to drop into the simmering stew. River and Woodchuck gave the hearts and livers to their Moms, who promptly put them on spits to roast over the fire.

The following day, the men went out hunting again. The women set about skinning the two deer and cutting up the meat. They separated and cleaned all the bones, to be used to make different tools. The sinews or tendons were saved and dried to make thread for sewing clothes. The cartilage from the joints would be cooked down to make glue. All parts of the deer were used; nothing went to waste. No life was taken randomly or uselessly.

As the younger boys worked on their tracking

skills, Red Dawn got his first deer that day with his new bow. His shot was straight and true, going into the deer's side, into the lung and heart. The deer went down and was gone instantly, and didn't suffer. This first kill had a deep impact on him, as he offered tobacco and prayed to the spirit of the deer, fighting back tears that burned to fall. River and Woodchuck just stood quietly, taking it all in. Everyone prayed with Red Dawn, while his Dad stood with his arm around his son's shoulder. They brought the deer back to the lodge, hanging it for the women to work on.

They went out three more times over the next few days, then decided to get one more deer before returning to the village. All the meat would be divided between their three families, with some set aside for Sachem Corn Tassel. Four deer would provide enough food for quite a while.

FROM BOY TO MAN

Singing Wolf, Rabbit, and Yellow Sky asked to meet with Tall Pine and Stands Strong. Red Dawn was growing into a young man now. He had taken his first deer with the bow and arrows he had made himself. He knew the woods and the animals, the waters and the weather. He was becoming a good hunter, fisherman, and shellfisherman. He had learned the skills to make his own tools and equipment from wood, bone, and stone. He could tan hides and make the tools to sew his own clothing. He knew where, when, and how to find different plants used for food, making cordage, and herbal medicines if he needed them. He could use fire to help take care of the land, to make boats, and to shape wood for bowls, spoons, and tools, as well as to keep warm and cook his food. He was a loving young man, caring and providing for his family. He was respectful and had participated and helped in many ceremonies.

After discussing it with him, his elders thought that next year Red Dawn would have enough skill to go out into the forest and support himself through the winter with all that he had learned. The experience of being by yourself out in Creation, depending on your own knowledge, insight, creativity, and skill, does far more than heighten physical skills. It generates intimacy with the Earth, the empathy and understanding of where the people's values emanate from, and knowing your place in the world.

BACK IN THE WINTER VILLAGE

While everyone had been away at the hunting lodge, Grandma Yellow Sky, Grandpa Singing Wolf, and Little Bird, Strawberry, and Punkinseed had stayed busy with all sorts of things. There was always the firewood, of course, to be collected. It was much easier to keep a big pile than to run low and have to go out in bad weather.

Strawberry and Punkinseed clamored for cooking lessons. So with Little Bird instructing them under Grandma's watchful eye, the two little girls put a kettle on to make soup. They carefully and intently scooped water from its jar into the kettle until it was half full. They added some dried corn and beans, with great discussion as to how much was enough for them all to have dinner. Little Bird stood right there as Strawberry built a fire under the kettle, taking a coal from the main fire to light it. Punkinseed tended the tiny blaze, keeping it fed with small branches and twigs.

Grandpas Singing Wolf and Rabbit came in with nine perch from the river. They had gone out ice fishing earlier in the day and brought in their catch for dinner. They cleaned the fish and got them roasting over the fire.

Once the soup was bubbling away, the girls mixed some cornmeal, hot water, dried blueberries, and sunflower seeds together for boiled bread, to cook in the soup. Punkinseed's cakes came out nice and firm, as she had mixed just enough hot water to hold the ingredients together. Strawberry, however, didn't quite have the equation figured out. She had added a bit too much water, and her "cakes" dissolved into thickening for the soup. Grandma calmly demonstrated adding just enough water to the cornmeal, showing her how to make sturdier dough. Some of the cornmeal always cooked off, which did add some thickening to the soup. A little cornmeal is fine, but not whole cakes, as Strawberry's had done. Well . . . they would have thickened the soup anyway. They just usually didn't have to cut soup with a knife!

Grandpas Singing Wolf and Rabbit had taken the girls out to give them some tracking lessons. Strawberry found some bird tracks in the snow, which she correctly identified as crow. Punkinseed followed some squirrel tracks right up to the tree where the squirrel was still sitting high on a branch. He looked down at the girls, gave them a mighty scolding, and scooted farther up the tree, out of sight. The girls laughed at his antics and, walking around the tree, could see his nest way up near the top. The little group walked on through the woods, calling out the tracks they saw: rabbit, skunk, raccoon, different smaller birds, mice, more squirrels, an occasional deer, otter, fisher, wolf, fox, bobcat, turkeys. The forest was very busy that day, with everybody coming out to find food and tend to their business. Singing Wolf and Rabbit showed the girls how the animals and birds all have habits and routines, trails, and nests in the same places, just like people do.

The Moms, Dads, cousins, and brothers had returned from the hunting trip. Their first stop was Corn Tassel's house to give her and her family some of the deer meat. They brought the rest home, and Smiling Dove, Blue Heron, and Stands Strong, with Yellow Sky and Little Bird, divided it up among their three families. They put most of the meat away, leaving some for dinner that evening. Everyone ate together that night, with a hearty (thick) soup and plenty of fresh, roasted deer meat.

Most winter evenings were spent around the fire. The grandparents had so many stories! There were stories of Moshop, the giant who came from the Creator to show the people how to live on the earth. There were stories of his wife Squant and their children; of Granny Squannit and her medicines. There were stories of times when Singing Wolf, Rabbit, and

Yellow Sky were young, the adventures they had, the people they met from so many other villages or nations. Rabbit told how he set out a snare trap, when he and Singing Wolf were boys. He told Singing Wolf that he was pretty sure he had caught a turkey and asked if he would go and check. Singing Wolf went to the trap, but there was no turkey. Rabbit had followed along silently. He made a sharp bird call right next to Singing Wolf's ear, who turned so quickly that he stepped into the snare, releasing its trigger. Singing Wolf was abruptly caught by the ankle, causing him to land squarely on his backside. Rabbit was also on the ground, holding his sides, laughing at the look on his friend's face. Now that they were elders, Singing Wolf could laugh and appreciate the humor of this "joke." Now that they were elders, Rabbit was still laughing so hard that he couldn't sit up straight!

So there were funny stories and scary stories. Teaching stories and history stories. Stories of earth and water, sun and sky, this world and others; of trees and plants; of eagles, hawks, and owls; of wolves and bears and mice. There were stories of the work of all those beings, and also of the humans. Grandpa Rabbit told his snare story as often as he could get away with it.

WINTER CEREMONIES

Soon came the time for Winter Ceremonies. Everyone in the villages gathered in the ceremonial longhouses. All of Green Pine came together at first light on the first morning. During the days that followed, the medicine people and the elders told the history of the people. They would tell how the earth was created and formed, how the mountains and the rocks, the trees and plants, the animals, birds, and fish all came to be.

The people heard about Moshop again and his relation to us, as he helped form the earth. People were reminded that the plants and the animals are

Moshop travels to Aquinnah
to take part in winter ceremonies.

our elders, as Creator made them before the humans. They heard how humans were made and had come from this earth. Creator gave all beings Original Instructions. For the humans, it was to keep the earth as it was created. People were given ceremony and prayer as ways to keep on this right path. People learned the ways of the animals and the plants and the waters and the stars, so that we could build our lives well, following our Original Instructions.

The Winter Ceremonies went on for several days. There was prayer and fasting, speaking and listening, special songs and silence. There were times when every person could speak what was on their mind or in their heart. In the evenings, there was feasting and dancing. Ceremony made a deep bond among all the people, nurturing love, cherishing family and all of Creation.

Everyone's heart and spirit were restored.

WINTER GOES BY

There were days of being inside with everyone when the snows and storms were blowing. Families visited back and forth in the longhouses, sharing meals and sharing stories. There was much laughter and games and no running in a house with a row of fires down the center!

And then there were days of sledding down snow-covered hills on old fur-worn deer hides or slide-skating on frozen rivers. Hot mint tea and stew never tasted so good as after a long day of sledding and sliding, fires warming up little bodies who, moving so fast over ice and snow, didn't realize how cold they had become.

Firewood was collected, hearty meals cooked, hides tanned for bedding or clothing. Bones of many animals were transformed into tool handles, needles, awls, arrowpoints, and hide scrapers. The families made one more trip to the hunting lodge, getting three deer this time. But that was all they needed. Like picking strawberries in the summer, some were left to ensure they would always be there.

Evenings were spent around the fires, talking, laughing, listening to stories, to the winter winds, and the fires crackling, spreading their warmth and comfort. While the storytelling was going on, the women showed the little girls how to get the fibers out of the milkweed and dogbane stalks, and hand spin or twist them into string and rope. Little Bird was already quite skilled at twisting cordage. The milkweed and dogbane were each different to work with, but she focused on increasing her skill with each. Little Bird and the women took turns showing the little girls, working slowly so they could learn by watching how it was done, and lending a hand when necessary, to assist tiny ones in their work.

The days were short, and the dark nights long. Little Bird loved the quiet stillness of winter nights. The family would go out for walks, especially when the moon was full and the light made a sparkling path across the frozen snow. Sometimes someone would catch the shape of an owl in flight, a shadow floating among the trees. They make no sound as they fly, the only evidence of their presence the screech of their prey when caught. The smallest of the kids understood this as part of Creator's plan.

CHAPTER 12

EDUCATION: A WAY OF LIFE OR ALLEGIANCE TO AN IDEAL?

WAMPANOAG EDUCATION

Traditional Wampanoag education, similar to that of other Indigenous societies, was based on relationship with the earth. Children were taught from the time they could walk, talk, observe, or think about the ways of the land, the waters, the skies, and all of Creation. They watched their parents and grandparents, learned by observing their elders, and were encouraged and guided when they showed an interest or aptitude.

Young people, like Little Bird and Strawberry,

learned how to feed themselves; clothe themselves; keep themselves warm in cold weather, cool in hot weather; and to heal themselves in sickness or injury. They learned how to gather materials and develop the skills to do all these things.

They could make the tools for hunting, fishing, house building, and boat building; for hide tanning, sewing, and gathering bulrush and cattail. They could make all household equipment and furnishings—dishes, clay cooking kettles, utensils, fire-starting tools, baskets, and mats.

They could grow the corn and other vegetables in the gardens; they knew where, when, and how to gather all the plants used in weaving bags, baskets, and mats; and they knew how to harvest the medicine and food plants.

They learned what trees grow in the homeland, what plants grow with those trees, and what animals live in those places. They learned the ways of the animals, their homes and trails and foods. And they learned how, where, and when to hunt.

They learned the waters, winds and currents, and to navigate by the stars when out on the open ocean. Boat-handling skills were needed to visit relatives on Capawack, Nantucket, or at Narragansett or Shinnecock. They knew when and where to catch ocean fish and shellfish, with hook and line, spear, dip net, seine net, weir, and trap. They fished in the freshwater rivers and lakes, and in the places that mix the salt and the fresh.

They learned that knowing the ways of the animals and fish, the plants and trees, is not just to be able to obtain them for food or other use, but to know them as fellow beings who share this earth with us, as relatives. They learned ceremony, prayer, and thanksgiving, to never take more than what was needed, to use everything taken, and to waste nothing.

Children knew their homeland, the landscape, and how to care for it as their ancestors had for countless generations. There are no words for "wild" or "wilderness" in our languages because the forests, the fields, the swamps, the marshes—the earth—are home. In respecting all the other beings of Creation, whether rock or tree, ant or beetle, water or wind, earth or deer, bear or moon, we respect ourselves. One does not happen without the other. Then life flourishes and is abundant. Needlessly or carelessly destroying the things of Creation, that which Creator made, was considered evil. Can you find one example of this relationship in each season of "When Life Was Our Own"?

EUROPEAN OR WESTERN EDUCATION

The English in the 1600s considered Wampanoag and other tribal nations backward and primitive. And judging from what was written in *Mourt's Relation,* that's the good news! In the chapter entitled "Reasons and Considerations touching the lawfulness of removing out of England into the parts of America," Mourt stated: "They are not industrious, neither have they art, science, skill or faculty to use either the land or the commodities of it. . . ." In other words the English were working really hard to justify coming to "America" and taking land that did not belong to them, as discussed in "Laws" in Chapter 10 of this book.

The English did not view the way Wampanoag people brought up children as "education." To the English, "education" happens when children sit in a classroom while a teacher relates information on different subjects to them, which the children then memorize. When the children have been through enough years of such education, after they have collected a sufficient amount of information, they graduate and receive a degree.

To this end, many of the Ivy League colleges in the East were started in the mid-1600s and included

"Indian schools." Harvard University in Cambridge, Massachusetts, was the first of these colleges to have a program for Indigenous students.

The Harvard Indian College was established in 1655 for the purpose of educating Native youth to European standards, to "reduce them to civility," to be like English people. The incentive to establish the Indian College was that Harvard would receive more funding from their financial sources in England.

Only five students ever attended the Indian College, three Nipmuc men from central Massachusetts and two Wampanoag men from the Aquinnah tribe on Martha's Vineyard. The Nipmucs were brothers Benjamin and Eleazar Larnell, who both died from malnutrition and their living conditions at the school; and James Wawaus, or Printer, so named because he worked in the college's printing press. James left school and returned home to Nipmuc country, the only one to continue living. The Wampanoag men were Joel Hiacoomes and Caleb Cheeshateaumuck. Joel was killed during a shipwreck just one month before graduation. Harvard would not grant him his degree even though he had completed his coursework, but did posthumously award it to him in 2011, the next time a Wampanoag person graduated from Harvard. Joel was the son of Hiacoomes, the first convert to Christianity mentioned earlier. Caleb was the only person to graduate, but he ultimately suffered the same fate as the Larnells. He graduated in 1666, dying just one year later from tuberculosis. He also became gravely ill from poor nutrition and living in a dank, cold, insufficiently heated building while a student.

Several years ago, in a presentation about Caleb Cheeshateaumuck, a guest speaker was exclaiming how wonderful it was that an Indigenous person had graduated from Harvard. That, of course, is a huge accomplishment for anyone. But why would a Wampanoag man in the 1660s need to go to Harvard? He already had received his Wampanoag education and could therefore fulfill all of his needs back in his home. Why did he need a Harvard education where he came to excel in Latin and Greek languages and studies? What was the benefit of learning these things?

Caleb, as many others in his time, wanted to obtain

This is a good imagining of what Caleb Cheeshateaumuck may have looked like.

this "education" to understand what English society was about. There was continued encroachment on Indigenous lands and increasing colonizing pressures on Indigenous people. Learning English ways allowed Native people to navigate in the white world, not to become like the English, but rather to adapt and survive the colonial changes in our world and save our own ways of life. This is a very critical point to remember.

LET'S THINK ABOUT THIS:

1. Is Wampanoag education actually education? Why or why not?

2. Do you think the statements made in *Mourt's Relation* about the Indigenous people not being industrious, or not having the science or skill to use the land, are accurate? How does "When Life Was Our Own" refute them?

3. When people graduate from a western education, are they fully able to maintain themselves? Does it enable them to survive in the society they live in?

CHAPTER 13

WHEN LIFE
WAS OUR OWN

ICE BEGINS TO MELT

Winter can seem very long when so much time is spent indoors. But finally the days were lengthening! Sometimes it was almost warm out, and the snows began to melt away. The light changed again, brighter and looking like spring. The buds on the trees and bushes were beginning to swell. The pines had an abundance of healthy new cones growing. Coming out of their dens and warrens and nests, the animals were beginning to move around more. One day the boys were out and about in the woods and ran home excitedly, as Woodchuck was sure he heard the first herring peepers!

One morning, everyone woke up to a sound. Strawberry blinked awake, trying to make out what that was . . . it was the river! The river was making a rushing sound! The ice had broken up and the water was moving. The snows and winds of winter were moving out, making room for the warm breath of spring. Pretty soon it would be time to start packing to go back to the planting fields. Then it would be time to get the herring. And so, the circle of seasons, the circle of life, begins again. Strawberry understood the seasons changing, but she didn't quite get the circle

Carrying on ancient ways, being out there with the ancestors.

idea. Undaunted nevertheless, she kept looking for it, figuring it was probably out in the woods somewhere.

On one especially warm day, Little Bird and Red Dawn walked to the river. It was still early, but maybe there was an early-riser herring making his way home to the pond. The sun was warm, the breeze was gentle, and it was coming up to New Year time, when all the world would begin again. Everything was new and fresh with the promise that new life brings.

EPILOGUE

THE TRUTH, TODAY

C hapter 8, in the "Reservations, Indian Districts, Land Allotments" section, ends with both the Mashpee and Aquinnah Wampanoag communities becoming towns in 1870. The following will briefly relate Wampanoag and Indigenous state history up to the present day.

Life changed drastically for Wampanoag and all Indigenous people in southern New England after King Philip's War of 1675. The patterns of encroachment and colonial restrictions continued through the rest of the 1600s, and into the 1700s and 1800s.

By the 1700s, the only Wampanoag communities that remained were:

Watuppa or Troy in Fall River
Betty's Neck on Assawompset Pond in Lakeville

Nemasket in Middleboro

Herring Pond or Manomet in south Plymouth

On Cape Cod:

Mashpee

Mattakeeset in Yarmouth

Punonakanit in Wellfleet

On Martha's Vineyard:

Gay Head or Aquinnah in Aquinnah

Deep Bottom or Nunnepog in Edgartown

Chappaquiddick

Christiantown in Takemmy, now West Tisbury

Nantucket

Over time, people in most of these communities died out, married non-Natives, or moved into other Wampanoag communities. 1870 brought another major change, with the transitioning of Mashpee and Aquinnah (then called Gay Head) from Indian Districts into towns. By the early twentieth century, the three most intact remaining communities were Mashpee, Aquinnah, and Herring Pond. Herring Pond is not a separate town, but became part of the town of Plymouth, Massachusetts. These three tribes have

Vernon with the kids, 1970s, down the bay, teaching the next generation.

both a traditional structure, with a chief and medicine person, as well as tribal council forms of governance. All three continue to live on the lands of their original villages. Through all the pressures of colonization, we were never removed from and never left these lands.

After 1870, Wampanoag people still largely lived by hunting, fishing, farming, and foraging. In the towns of Mashpee and Aquinnah, Wampanoag people were the only ones who were the selectmen or town administrators. That began to change by the 1960s, when more and more non-Native people bought land and moved in. Because these two towns had been reservations for so long, they did not develop as fast as the others around them, remaining forested with pristine beaches. This made them "prime real estate": The land was greatly desired by outside people because through buying and reselling it, they could make a lot of money. Housing and business development created drastic changes. Huge areas of forest continue to be cut down, waters polluted, and access to traditional hunting, fishing, or foraging areas restricted by private property or development. In each town, Wampanoag people make up approximately 10 to 15 percent of the population. Mashpee has 170 acres in the town of Mashpee; Aquinnah has just under 500 acres in that town. These are tiny parcels compared to original village days, or even District days.

Tribal nations that continue to live on traditional homelands, or those they were removed to, can achieve either state or federal recognition. This provides legal status to support our continued existence as distinct nations and cultures, given the ravages of colonization. As Indigenous people, we are not another racial or ethnic minority. Federal or state recognition is acknowledgment of Indigenous people as sovereign nations who experienced near destruction.

There are criteria to be met for either status. For tribes petitioning for federal recognition, this includes having a land base and being able to establish family genealogies. How this last is done varies from tribe to tribe and state to state.

Both Mashpee and Aquinnah are now federally recognized tribes as of 2007 and 1987 respectively. They have a government-to-government relationship with the federal government of the United States. They receive funding, programs, and services to assist tribal citizens. Tribal governments are organized into Administration, Health, Human Services, Education, Tribal Historic Preservation and Cultural Services, Natural Resources, Membership and Enrollment, and Planning departments. The Stockbridge-Munsee of Wisconsin, formerly the Mahican of the western end of Massachusetts, are federally recognized as well.

In Massachusetts, the criteria for state recognition are under development, even though there are those with that designation. Herring Pond Wampanoag and the Nipmuc are state recognized tribes, defining them as tribal nations within the state.

The Indigenous tribes within the state of Massachusetts are the Pennacook (part of the Abenaki), from the northern part of the state where it borders New Hampshire; the Nipmuc, who still maintain their original homeland in the middle of the state; the Pocumtuk from the western part of the state; and the Mahican (Stockbridge-Munsee) near the border of New York; and the Wampanoag in the east.

The Indigenous people in the rest of what is now

southern New England are the Abenaki—while from Vermont and New Hampshire, their original homelands reach into what is now Massachusetts; the Narragansett and Niantic in Rhode Island; and the Pequot and Mohegan in Connecticut.

Each of these communities continues to maintain strong cultural and kinship ties within themselves and with the other tribal people in southern New England. We are still here.

We have been on quite a journey in this book, and traveled through some tough history. Each aspect of our definition of racism has, unfortunately, been met.

We are still here.

While, again, this is not about blaming anyone, we all have responsibility in this history. None of us can change what happened in the past. But we can learn the truth of history, and how people and the earth were affected in damaging, hurtful, unfair ways. We can take that learning to heart so that going forward is done in good and respectful ways. We can create the promise of new life. What can we do to make that happen?

RESOURCES FOR YOUNG READERS

Aliki. *Corn Is Maize: The Gift of the Indians.* New York: HarperCollins, 1976.

Bandes, Hanna, and Jeanette Winter. *Sleepy River.* New York: Philomel, 1993.

Benton-Banai, Edward (Ojibway). *The Mishomis Book.* Minneapolis: University of Minnesota Press, 2010.

Bruchac, Joseph (Abenaki), Jonathan London, and Thomas Locker. *Thirteen Moons on Turtle's Back.* New York: Penguin Young Readers Group, 1992.

Bruchac, Marge (Abenaki), and William Maughan. *Malian's Song.* Middlebury, VT: Vermont Folklife Center, 2005.

Cherry, Lynne. *A River Ran Wild.* New York: Clarion, 2002.

Coombs, Linda (Aquinnah Wampanoag). *Powwow.* Modern Curriculum Press, 1992.

Francis, Lee DeCora (Penobscot/Ho-Chunk), and Susan Drucker. *Kunu's Basket: A Story from Indian Island.* Thomaston, ME: Tilbury House Publishers, 2015.

Grace, Catherine O'Neill, and Marge Bruchac (Abenaki). *1621: A New Look at Thanksgiving.* Washington, DC: National Geographic Kids, 2004.

Hunter, Sally M., and Joe Allen. *Four Seasons of Corn: A Winnebago Tradition.* Minneapolis: Lerner Publishing Group, 1996.

Jennings, Paulla (Narragansett), and Ramona Peters (Mashpee Wampanoag). *Strawberry Thanksgiving.* Modern Curriculum Press, 1992.

Koller, Jackie French, and Marcia Sewall. *Nickommoh! A Thanksgiving Celebration.* New York: Atheneum, 1999.

Ortiz, Simon J. (Acoma Pueblo), and Sharol Graves. *The People Shall Continue.* New York: Lee & Low, 1977.

Peters, Robert (Mashpee Wampanoag). *Da Goodie Monsta.* Cambridge, MA: Wiggles Press, 2009.

Peters, Russell M. (Mashpee Wampanoag). *Clambake: A Wampanoag Tradition.* Minneapolis: Lerner Publishing Group, 1992.

Regguinti, Gordon, and Dale Kakkak. *The Sacred Harvest: Ojibway Wild Rice Gathering.* Minneapolis: Lerner Publishing Group, 1992.

Savageau, Cheryl (Abenaki), and Robert Hynes. *Muskrat Will Be Swimming.* Gardiner, ME: Tilbury House Publishers, 1996.

Sockabasin, Allen (Passamaquoddy), and Rebekah Raye. *Thanks to the Animals.* Gardiner, ME: Tilbury House Publishers, 2014.

Soctomah, Donald (Passamaquoddy), and Jean Flahive. *Remember Me: Tomah Joseph's Gift to Franklin Roosevelt.* Gardiner, ME: Tilbury House Publishers, 2015.

Swamp, Chief Jake (Mohawk), and Erwin Printup Jr. *Giving Thanks: A Native American Good Morning Message.* New York: Lee & Low, 1997.

Waters, Kate, and Russ Kendall. *Tapenum's Day.* New York: Scholastic Press, 1996.

Wittstock, Laura Waterman, and Dale Kakkak. *Ininatig's Gift of Sugar: Traditional Native Sugarmaking.* Minneapolis: Lerner Publishing Group, 1993.

BIBLIOGRAPHY

PRIMARY SOURCES
PLYMOUTH SETTLEMENT

Altham, Emmanuel, John Pory, and Isaack de Rasieres. *Three Visitors to Early Plymouth.* Edited by Sydney V. James Jr.

Bradford, William. *Of Plymouth Plantation: 1620–1647.* Edited by Samuel Eliot Morison. 2001.

Goddard, Ives, and Kathleen Bragdon. *Native Writings in Massachusett.* Vols. I & II.

Heath, Dwight B., ed. *Mourt's Relation: A Journal of the Pilgrims at Plymouth,* 1622. Bedford, MA: Applewood Books, 1963.

Josselyn, John. *An Account of Two Voyages to New England.* Boston: William Veazie, 1865.

———. *New Englands Rarities Discovered.* 1672.

Morton, Thomas. *New English Canaan.* 1637.

Verrazano, Giovanni. *Sailors Narratives of Voyages Along the New England Coast, 1524–1624.* Edited by George Parker Winship, 1905.

Williams, Roger. *A Key Into the Language of America.* 1643. 4th ed. J. Hammond Trumbull, 1973.

Wood, William. *New England Prospect.* 1634.

CHRISTOPHER COLUMBUS

Las Casas, Bartolomé. *The Devastation of the Indies.*

SECONDARY SOURCES
PLYMOUTH SETTLEMENT/ COLONIZATION/HISTORY

Brooks, Lisa (Abenaki). *The Common Pot: The Recovery of Native Space in the Northeast.* Minneapolis: University of Minnesota Press, 2008.

Bross, Kristina. *Dry Bones and Indian Sermons: Praying Indians in Colonial America.* Ithaca, NY: Cornell University Press, 2004.

Cronon, William. *Changes in the Land: Indians, Colonists, and the Ecology of New England.* New York: Hill and Wang, 1983, 2003.

Dunbar-Ortiz, Roxanne (Cherokee). *An Indigenous Peoples' History of the United States.* Boston: Beacon Press, 2014.

———. *An Indigenous Peoples' History of the United States for Young People.* Adapted by Jean Mendoza and Debbie Reese. Boston: Beacon Press, 2020.

Jennings, Francis. *The Invasion of America: Indians, Colonialism, and the Cant of Conquest.* Chapel Hill: The University of North Carolina Press, 1975.

Newell, Margaret Ellen. *Brethren by Nature: New England Indians, Colonists, and the Origins of American Slavery.* Ithaca, NY: Cornell University Press, 2015.

O'Brien, Jean M. (Ojibway). *Dispossession by Degrees: Indian Land and Identity in Natick, Massachusetts, 1650–1790.* Cambridge, UK: Cambridge University Press, 1997.

———. *Firsting and Lasting: Writing Indians Out of Existence in New England.* Minneapolis: University of Minnesota Press, 2010.

Russell, Howard S. *Indian New England Before the Mayflower.* Hanover, NH: University Press of New England, 1980.

Salisbury, Neal. *Manitou and Providence: Indians, Europeans, and the Making of New England, 1500–1643*. New York: Oxford University Press, 1982.

Salisbury, Neal, and Colin G. Calloway. *Reinterpreting New England Indians and the Colonial Experience*. Colonial Society of Massachusetts, 2005.

Sleeper-Smith, Susan, and Juliana Barr, Jean M. O'Brien (Ojibway), Nancy Shoemaker, Scott Manning Stevens, ed. *Why You Can't Teach United States History Without American Indians*. Chapel Hill: The University of North Carolina Press, 2015.

Speck, Frank Gouldsmith. *Territorial Subdivisions and Boundaries of the Wampanoag, Massachusett, and Nauset Indians*. Indian Notes and Monographs. Museum of the American Indian, Heye Foundation, 1928.

Young, Alexander. *Chronicles of the Pilgrim Fathers*. Boston: Charles C. Little and James Brown, 1841.

Zinn, Howard. *A People's History of the United States*. Teaching Edition. New York: Harper, 1980, 1995, 1998, 1990, 2003.

PRIMARY SOURCES

KING PHILIP'S WAR

Church, Benjamin. *Diary of King Philip's War, 1675–1676*. Little Compton Historical Society, 1975.

Church, Thomas. *The History of Philip's War. As Originally Published in 1827*. Edited by Samuel G. Drake. Scituate, MA: Digital Scanning Inc., 1999.

Folsom, James K. *So Dreadfull A Judgement: Puritan Responses to King Philip's War 1676–1677*. Edited by Richard Slotkin. Middletown, CT: Wesleyan University Press, 1979.

Rowlandson, Mary. *The Sovereignty and Goodness of God: The Captivity of Mary Rowlandson*. Edited by Neal Salisbury. Originally published in 1682. Boston: Bedford/St. Martin's, 2018.

SECONDARY SOURCES

KING PHILIP'S WAR

Brooks, Lisa (Abenaki). *Our Beloved Kin: A New History of King Philip's War*. New Haven, CT: Yale University Press, 2018.

Calloway, Colin G., ed. *After King Philip's War: Presence and Persistence in Indian New England*. Hanover, NH: University Press of New England, 1997.

DeLucia, Christine M. *Memory Lands: King Philip's War and the Place of Violence in the Northeast*. New Haven, CT: Yale University Press, 2018.

Drake, James D. *King Philip's War: Civil War in New England, 1675–1676*. Amherst, MA: University of Massachusetts Press, 1999.

Lepore, Jill. *The Name of War: King Philip's War and the Origins of American Identity*. New York: Vintage Books, 1999.

Mandell, Daniel R. *King Philip's War: Colonial Expansion, Native Resistance, and the End of Indian Sovereignty*. Baltimore: The Johns Hopkins University Press, 2010.

Schultz, Eric B., and Michael J. Tougias. *King Philip's War: The History and Legacy of America's Forgotten Conflict*. New York: The Countryman Press, 2000.

WAMPANOAG/NEW ENGLAND NATIVE AUTHORS

Avant, Joan Tavares (Mashpee Wampanoag). *People of the First Light: Wisdoms of a Mashpee Wampanoag Elder*. Mashpee, MA: Joan Tavares Avant, 2010.

Mills, Earl, Sr. (Mashpee Wampanoag). *Talking with the Elders of Mashpee: Memories of Earl H. Mills, Sr.* 2012.

Mills, Earl, Sr. (Mashpee Wampanoag), and Alicja Mann. *Son of Mashpee: Reflections of Chief Flying Eagle, A Wampanoag*. 2006.

Mills, Earl, Sr. (Mashpee Wampanoag), and Betty Breen. *Cape Cod Wampanoag Cookbook: Wampanoag Indian Recipes, Images & Lore*. Santa Fe: Clear Light Publishers, 2001.

Peters, Paula (Mashpee Wampanoag). *Mashpee Nine: A Story of Cultural Justice.* Smokesygnals, 2016.

Peters, Russell M. (Mashpee Wampanoag). *The Wampanoags of Mashpee: An Indian Perspective on American History.* R.M. Peters, 1987.

Senier, Siobhan, ed. *Dawnland Voices: An Anthology of Indigenous Writing from New England.* Lincoln, NE: University of Nebraska Press, 2014.

Vanderhoop, Jannette (Aquinnah Wampanoag). *People of the First Light.* Aquinnah Cultural Center, 2009.

ANALYSIS OF WRITTEN MATERIAL

Dunbar-Ortiz, Roxanne (Cherokee), and Dina Gilio-Whitaker. *All the Real Indians Died Off.* Boston: Beacon Press, 2016.

Loewen, James W. *Lies My Teacher Told Me: Everything Your American History Textbook Got Wrong.* New York: The New Press, 1995.

Mihesuah, Devon A. (Choctaw). *American Indians: Stereotypes & Realities.* Atlanta: Clarity Press, 1996.

National Museum of the American Indian. *Do All Indians Live in Tipis?* 2nd ed. Washington, DC: Smithsonian Books, 2018.

Reese, Debbie (Nambé Pueblo). American Indians in Children's Literature. americanindiansinchildrensliterature.blogspot.com/.

Slapin, Beverly, and Doris Seale (Santee Lakota). *A Broken Flute.* Oyate Press, 2005.

———. *Through Indian Eyes: The Native Experience in Books for Children.* Oyate Press, 1991.

DECOLONIZATION

d'Errico, Peter P. *Federal Anti-Indian Law: The Legal Entrapment of Indigenous Peoples.* Santa Barbara: Praeger, 2022.

Geniusz, Wendy Makoons (Anishinaabe). *Our Knowledge Is Not Primitive: Decolonizing Botanical Anishinaabe Teachings.* Syracuse, NY: Syracuse University Press, 2009.

Lonetree, Amy (Ho-Chunk). *Decolonizing Museums: Representing Native America in National and Tribal Museums.* Chapel Hill, NC: The University of North Carolina Press, 2012.

Mihesuah, Devon Abbott (Choctaw). *Indigenous American Women: Decolonization, Empowerment, Activism.* Lincoln, NE: University of Nebraska Press, 2003.

———, ed. *Natives and Academics: Researching and Writing About American Indians.* Lincoln, NE: University of Nebraska Press, 1998.

———. *Recovering Our Ancestors' Gardens: Indigenous Recipes and Guide to Diet and Fitness.* Lincoln, NE: University of Nebraska Press, 2005.

Simpson, Leanne Betasamosake (Anishinaabe). *As We Have Always Done: Indigenous Freedom Through Radical Resistance.* Minneapolis, MN: University of Minnesota Press, 2017.

Tuhiwai Smith, Linda (Maori). *Decolonizing Methodologies: Research and Indigenous Peoples.* London: Zed Books, 2012.

GENERAL READING/CULTURAL

Anderson, Kim, and Maria Campbell, Christi Belcourt, eds. *Keetsahnak: Our Missing and Murdered Indigenous Sisters.* Edmonton, Alberta: The University of Alberta Press, 2018.

Anderson, M. Kat. *Tending the Wild: Native American Knowledge and the Management of California's Natural Resources.* Berkeley, CA: University of California Press, 2005.

Barreiro, Jose, ed. (Taino). "Indian Corn of the Americas: Gift to the World." *Northeast Indian Quarterly* (Spring/Summer 1989).

Beresford-Kroeger, Diana. *The Global Forest: 40 Ways Trees Can Save Us.* New York: Viking, 2010.

———. *To Speak for the Trees: My Life's Journey from Ancient Celtic Wisdom to a Healing Vision of the Forest.* Portland, OR: Timber Press, 2019.

Cajete, Gregory (Tewa). *Native Science: Natural Laws of Interdependence.* Santa Fe: Clear Light Publishers, 2000.

———, ed. *A People's Ecology: Explorations in Sustainable Living.* Santa Fe: Clear Light Publishers, 1999.

Deloria, Vine, Jr. (Lakota). *The World We Used to Live In.* Golden, CO: Fulcrum Publishing, 2006.

George-Kanentiio, Douglas M. (Mohawk). "Origins." Chap. 1 in *Iroquois on Fire: A Voice from the Mohawk Nation.* Lincoln, NE: University of Nebraska Press, 2008.

Gilio-Whitaker, Dina. *As Long As Grass Grows: The Indigenous Fight for Environmental Justice, from Colonization to Standing Rock.* Boston: Beacon Press, 2019.

Kimmerer, Robin Wall (Potawatomi). *Braiding Sweetgrass.* Minneapolis: Milkweed Editions, 2013.

———. *Gathering Moss.* Corvallis, OR: Oregon State University Press, 2003.

LaDuke, Winona (Ojibway). *All Our Relations: Native Struggles for Land and Life.* Chicago: Haymarket Books, 1999.

Mihesuah, Devon A. (Choctaw), and Elizabeth Hoover (Mohawk). *Indigenous Food Sovereignty in the United States: Restoring Cultural Knowledge, Protecting Environments and Regaining Health.* Norman, OK: University of Oklahoma Press, 2019.

Mitchell, Sherri (Penobscot). *Sacred Instructions.* Berkeley, CA: North Atlantic Books, 2018.

Nelson, Melissa K., ed. (Ojibway). *Original Instructions: Indigenous Teachings for a Sustainable Future.* Rochester, VT: Bear & Company, 2008.

Peacock, Thomas D. (Ojibwe). *The Wolf's Trail: An Ojibwe Story, Told by Wolves.* Duluth, MN: Holy Cow! Press, 2020.

Versluis, Arthur. *Sacred Earth: The Spiritual Landscape of Native America.* Rochester, VT: 1992.

IMAGE CREDITS